Part B

The Cambridge English Course

This book contains the second third of the complete edition of *The Cambridge English Course,* Student's Book 2.

D1789284

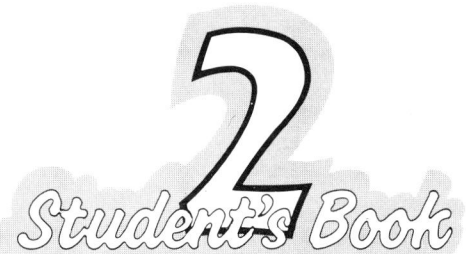

2

Student's Book

Michael Swan and Catherine Walter

Cambridge University Press

Cambridge

New York   New Rochelle   Melbourne   Sydney

The right of the University of Cambridge to print and sell all manner of books was granted by Henry VIII in 1534. The University has printed and published continuously since 1584.

Published by the Press Syndicate of the University of Cambridge
The Pitt Building, Trumpington Street, Cambridge CB2 1RP
32 East 57th Street, New York, NY 10022, USA
10 Stamford Road, Oakleigh, Melbourne 3166, Australia

© Cambridge University Press 1985, 1986

Complete edition first published 1985
This split edition first published 1986
Fourth printing 1988

Designed by John Youé and Associates, Croydon, Surrey
Typeset by Text Filmsetters Limited, London
Origination by BTA Reprographics Limited, London
Printed in Great Britain by W. S. Cowell Ltd, Ipswich

ISBN 0 521 28984 X Student's Book 2

Split edition:
ISBN 0 521 33757 7 Part A
ISBN 0 521 33758 5 Part B
ISBN 0 521 33759 3 Part C

ISBN 0 521 28982 3 Teacher's Book 2
ISBN 0 521 28983 1 Practice Book 2
ISBN 0 521 31626 X Test Book 2
ISBN 0 521 24817 5 Cassette Set 2
ISBN 0 521 30324 9 Student's Cassette 2

Authors' acknowledgements

We are grateful to all the people who have helped us with this book. Our thanks to:

The many people whose ideas have influenced our work, including all the colleagues and students from whom we have learnt.

Ruth Gairns, Stuart Redman, Alan Duff, Alan Maley, Mario Rinvolucri and Penny Ur, for specific ideas and exercises we have borrowed.

Those institutions and teachers who were kind enough to work with the Pilot Edition of this course, and whose comments have done so much to shape the final version.

Peter Roach for his expert and sensible help with the phonetic transcription.

John Youé, Jack Wood, Margaret Dodd, Tanya Ball, Alison Pincott, Jane Molineaux, Jason Youé and Helen Lawrence of John Youé and Associates, for their invaluable help in the design and production of the book.

John and Angela Eckersley, and the staff of the Eckersley School of English, Oxford, for making it possible for us to try out the Pilot Edition of the course in their classrooms.

Ken Blissett, John and Rita Peake, Alexandra Phillips, Pat Robbins, Sue Ward, Adrian Webber, Jane and Keith Woods, for agreeing to be questioned within earshot of our microphones.

Mark, for all his help and support.

And finally, to Adrian du Plessis, Peter Donovan, Jeanne McCarten and Peter Ducker of Cambridge University Press, for their creativity, their understanding, and their outstanding professional competence.

Michael Swan   Catherine Walter

The authors and publishers would like to thank the following people and institutions for their help in testing the material and for the invaluable feedback which they provided:

The British Council, Thessaloniki, Greece; The British School, Florence, Italy; Australian College of English, Sydney, Australia; University of Berne, Berne, Switzerland; Etudes Pedagogiques de l'Enseignement Secondaire, Geneva, Switzerland; The Bell School, Cambridge; Bell College, Saffron Walden; Oxford Language Centre, Oxford; The British Institute, Rome, Italy; The Newnham Language Centre, Cambridge; Adult Migrant Education Services, Melbourne, Australia; Communication in Business, Paris, France; Studio School of English, Cambridge; International House, Arezzo, Italy; Grange School, Santiago, Chile; Eurocentre, Cambridge; Gillian Porter-Ladousse, Paris, France; Pauline Bramall, Karlsruhe, W. Germany; College de Saussure, Geneva, Switzerland; Noreen O'Shea, Paris, France; Eurocentre, Brighton; New School of English, Cambridge; Eckersley School, Oxford; Central School of English, London; Anglo-Continental School, Bournemouth; Godmer House School of English, Oxford; School of English Studies, Folkestone; Davies's School of English, London; Oxford Language Centre, Oxford; Regent School, Rome, Italy; Brunswick Education Centre, Victoria, Australia.

Contents

Note

Page numbering from the complete edition of Student's Book 2 has been retained throughout.

Map of Book 2*

In Unit	FUNCTIONS AND SKILLS Students will learn to	NOTIONS, TOPICS AND SITUATIONS Students will learn to talk about
12	Ask for explanations; describe processes; express doubt and certainty.	Manufacturing and other processes; causes of past events.
13	Ask for and give directions; describe; define.	Landscapes; towns; houses; objects.
14	Ask about and express preferences; connect written text; express agreement and disagreement.	Relatives; family life.
15	Express wants, hopes and intentions; ask for favours; agree to requests; thank and reply to thanks.	Jobs; leisure activities.
16	Express opinions; negotiate.	Personal expenditure; budgets; quantity.
17	Narrate; ask for and give information; link written texts.	Time relations; habits.
18	Express opinions; report; use dictionaries when reading.	History; scientific discoveries; probability.
19	Make small talk: greet; welcome; ask for and give opinions; ask for repetition; take leave.	Job routines; food; entertainment.
20	Give instructions; give opinions; suggest; persuade; warn.	Housework; plans; the notion of orientation; personal problems.
21	Express preferences, opinion and obligation; complain.	Electrical appliances; breakdowns in common possessions.
REVISION 22	Use what they have learnt in different ways.	No new topics.

*This 'map' of the course should be translated into students' language where possible.

VOCABULARY: Students will learn about 1,000 common words and expressions during the course.

GRAMMAR	PHONOLOGY
Students will learn or revise these grammar points	**Students will study these aspects of pronunciation**
Simple present passive; past passive; present and past participles; question forms.	Hearing /ə/; /h/; decoding rapid speech.
Imperatives; *there is/are*; *feel/smell* + adjective; relative pronouns and their omission; preposition at end of clause.	Decoding rapid speech; /i:/, /ɪ/ and /aɪ/; pronunciations of the letter *i*.
Would rather; *should*.	Linking with /r/, /j/, and /w/; sentence stress.
Want, would like, and *would love*; *want* + object + infinitive; *hope/going/try to*; *I/We wondered if* + past.	/əʊ/; decoding rapid speech.
Must and *can*; quantifiers; *will* for proposals; *too/enough to*...	Linking, liaison and assimilation.
Time clauses with *as soon as*, *before*, *after*, *until*; *still, yet, already*; *such* and *so*; past perfect.	/ɒ/, /ɔ:/, /əʊ/ and their spellings; decoding rapid speech.
Reported speech; *used to*; word order in reported questions; modals; *likely*; *say* and *tell*.	Rhythm; initial consonant clusters beginning with *s*.
Question-tags; prepositions in questions; *so/neither (do I)*.	Intonation of question tags; fluency practice.
Infinitive of purpose; *by . . . ing*; *had better*; negative imperatives; hypothetical conditions; *ought to*; *Let's*; *Why don't*.	Consonant clusters with *ex*, final consonant clusters.
Should; phrasal verbs; present tenses; simple past; *won't* = refuses to.	Spellings of final /ə/; decoding fast speech.
General revision.	Exceptions to general rules about spelling/pronunciation links; fluency practice.

Paper-making centuries ago

Causes and origins

A From tree to paper

1 Read the text with a dictionary, and put one of these words into each blank: *paper, wood, trees.* Ask the teacher for help if necessary.

Excuse me. What does 'invented' mean?

Excuse me. I don't understand this.

Excuse me. Can you explain this word?

Excuse me. How do you pronounce this?

Wood fibres magnified

......1...... was invented by the Chinese in the first century AD. The art of ......2......-making took 700 years to reach the Muslim world and another 700 years to get to Britain (via Spain, southern France and Germany).

Most ......3...... is made from ......4....... When ......5...... are cut down, they are transported by land or water to paper mills. Here they are cut up and the ......6...... is broken up into fibres, which are mixed with water and chemicals. This ......7...... pulp is then dried on a machine and made into ......8.......

Paper-making today

Future paper

......9......-making is an important British industry, and ......10...... from Britain is exported to South Africa, Australia and many other countries. Some of the ......11...... used in the British paper-making industry comes from ......12...... grown in Britain, but ......13...... is also imported from other countries such as Norway. One tree is needed for every 400 copies of a typical forty-page newspaper. If half the adults in Britain each buy one daily ......14......, this uses up over 40,000 ......15...... a day. ......16...... are being cut down faster than they are being replaced, so there may be a serious paper shortage before the year 2000.

2 Close your book and listen to the sentences. Are they true or false?

3 The word *America* (/əˈmerɪkə/) has the sound /ə/ twice. Which ten of the following words also contain the sound /ə/?

iron century paper
correct Germany adults
fibre replaced pulp
machine industry exported
Africa countries Norway
needed serious shortage

4 Make some true sentences.

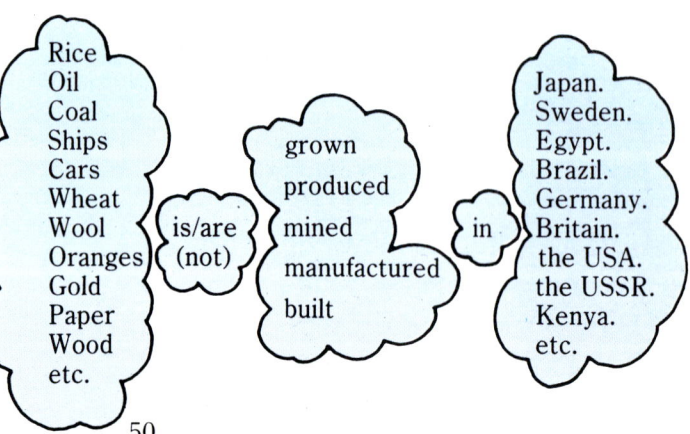

Rice Oil Coal Ships Cars Wheat Wool Oranges Gold Paper Wood etc.	is/are (not)	grown produced mined manufactured built	in	Japan. Sweden. Egypt. Brazil. Germany. Britain. the USA. the USSR. Kenya. etc.

Legend:
- WOOD
- PAPER
- WHEAT
- RICE
- MAIZE
- ORANGES
- SHIPS
- CARS
- AIRCRAFT
- COAL
- NATURAL GAS
- OIL
- GOLD
- SILVER
- COPPER
- IRON
- SALT
- GLASS

5 Look at the map. Then listen to the recording and answer the questions. Examples:

True or false? Oil is produced in Texas.

True.

Is wheat grown in Arizona?

No, it isn't.

6 Think of a country. Write four sentences about it; use verbs from Exercise 4 in three of the sentences.
Read your sentences to some other students. They will try to guess the country; you can help them if you want. Example:

Wool is produced there. Coal is mined there. Paper is manufactured there. Some good Olympic runners have come from there.

Is it the USA?   *No, it's in Europe.*

Is it East Germany?   *No.*

Britain?   *Yes.*

7 Work in groups. See which group can finish the questions fastest. Use your dictionaries if you need to.
Write the name of:

1. something made of wood that you can play a game with
2. something made of iron that is found in a house
3. something made of china
4. something made of plastic that helps you buy things
5. something made of glass that helps you see
6. something made of leather that you can carry things in
7. something made of wool that people wear on their feet
8. something in the classroom that's made of steel
9. something made of cotton that someone in the group is wearing
10. something made of synthetic fibre that someone in the group is wearing

B Who killed Harrison?

1 Grammar. Look at the examples. Then write the infinitives and past participles of the verbs below.

INFINITIVE:	Can you **make** an omelette? I want **to see** the manager. We need **to import** less.
PAST TENSE:	She **made** that dress herself. I **saw** Alan yesterday. We **imported** 4m tons last year.
PAST PARTICIPLE	I've **made** you a cake. I haven't **seen** her today. We have **imported** more this year. Paper is **made** from wood. He was last **seen** in Cairo. This was **imported** from Taiwan.

1. know   steal   go   drink
2. find   build   think
3. mix   question   kill   arrest   need   export
4. manufacture   use   dry

2 Put the *-ing* form or the past participle.

1. 'What are you doing?' 'I'm .... bread.' (*make*)
2. Paper is .... from wood. (*make*)
3. When was that church ....?(*build*)
4. Mary and John are .... their own house. (*build*)
5. Why are you .... up that chair? (*break*)
6. I think the window was .... by a stone. (*break*)
7. Too many trees are .... down every year. (*cut*)
8. When we arrived, she was .... his hair. (*cut*)
9. The police are .... him now. (*question*)
10. When she was ...., she said nothing. (*question*)

7 Read the following text, but do *not* look at the text on the opposite page. Then work with a partner, and ask him or her questions to get more complete information about Harrison's death.

HARRISON was last seen alive at 9.30 p.m. (*Where?*) He was found dead in his flat by his wife Mary when she came home from a dance. (*What time?*) He was killed with a revolver. A small French-English dictionary was found by his body. (*Anything else? Was anything stolen?*)

The police suspect Haynes, MacHale and Cannon. All three were arrested the next morning.

HAYNES once worked for Harrison, but was sacked. (*Why?*) He has often said he hates Harrison, and would like to kill him. He was seen by three witnesses at 10.30. (*Where?*) When he was arrested, a revolver was found in his car. (*Where were his fingerprints found?*)

MacHALE is known to the police as a thief, but not as a killer. (*Where is he from?*) He is an old friend of Harrison's. (*Does he know Mrs Harrison?*) When he was arrested, £2,000 in cash was found in his wallet. (*Anything else?*)

CANNON works in an import-export business. (*Where?*) Harrison owed him a lot of money. When he was questioned, he said that he was at his hotel from 9.30 to 11.30. (*What did his wife say?*) He was seen earlier coming out of Harrison's flat. (*What time?*) Cannon's wife is an old friend of Mary Harrison's.

WHO DO YOU THINK KILLED HARRISON?

52

3 Make some true sentences.

I think
I'm sure
I know
Perhaps

America   the Taj Mahal
J.F. Kennedy   *Psycho*
the *Pastoral Symphony*
paper   TV   radium
Everest   *Hamlet*
the *Communist Manifesto*
the 1974 World Cup

was

won
built
written
directed
discovered
first climbed
invented
killed

by

Beethoven   Baird   Columbus
Marx and Engels   West Germany
Pierre and Marie Curie   Oswald
Shakespeare   Shah Jehan
the Chinese   Hitchcock
Hillary and Tensing

in

1963   1808   1898   1953
1600   1848   1923
1492   the first century

Now listen to the recording.

4 Who, what, when, where, why, how?
Listen to the answers and write the
question-words. Examples:

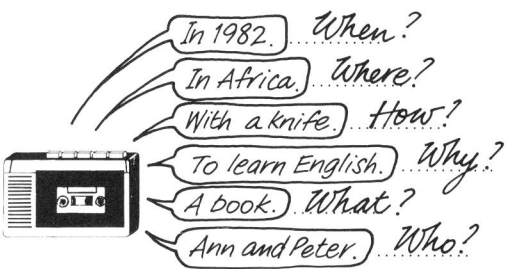

In 1982.   *When?*
In Africa.   *Where?*
With a knife.   *How?*
To learn English.   *Why?*
A book.   *What?*
Ann and Peter.   *Who?*

5 Make questions.

1. Gloria gets up very early. ('*What time...?*')
2. The church was built by Wren. ('*When...?*')
3. I'm waiting. ('*What...?*')
4. He was sacked last week. ('*Why...?*')
5. We're going on holiday in July. ('*Where...?*')
6. I don't usually sit here. ('*Where...?*')
7. He never travels by car. ('*How...?*')
8. My father was killed when I was six.
   ('*How...?*')

6 Pronunciation. Pronounce these words.

here   half   home   Harrison   hated   who
hand   hungry   happy

Listen and write what you hear.

7 Read the following text, but do *not* look at the text on the opposite page. Then work with a
partner, and ask him or her questions to get more complete information about Harrison's death.

HARRISON was last seen alive talking to a woman in the street outside his flat in
central London. (*What time?*) He was found dead by his wife (*Name?*) when she
came home from a dance at 11.30. (*How was he killed?*) A Paris underground
ticket was found by his body. (*Anything else?*) His wallet had been stolen.

The police suspect Haynes, MacHale and Cannon. All three were
arrested the next morning.

HAYNES once worked for Harrison, but was sacked for stealing.
He has often said he hates Harrison, and would like
to kill him. He was seen by three witnesses 50km
from Harrison's home. (*What time?*) His fingerprints
were found in Harrison's flat. When he was arrested,
his car was searched by the police. (*Was anything found?*)

MacHALE is from Scotland. He is a very old friend of Mrs Harrison's. (*Did he
know Mr Harrison?*) When he was arrested, a love letter (signed '*Mary*') was found in his
pocket. (*Anything else? Find out if MacHale is known to the police.*)

CANNON works in Paris. (*What does he do? Find out if he owed Harrison money.*)
He was seen coming out of Harrison's flat at 9.15. When his wife
was questioned, she said that he was out of his hotel all evening.
(*What did he say? Find out if Cannon's wife knows Mary Harrison.*)

WHO DO YOU THINK KILLED HARRISON?

53

Descriptions

A Places

1 Look at the picture. Which word goes with which number?

hill mountain valley wood stream
waterfall island river lake bridge
path road

2 How do you get from A to B? Use the words in Exercise 1 with these prepositions.

across through along up down

Example: 'You go down the hill, . . .'

3 Look at the map and listen to the recording. Decide whether the sentences are true or false. Example:

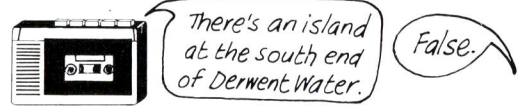

There's an island at the south end of Derwent Water. False.

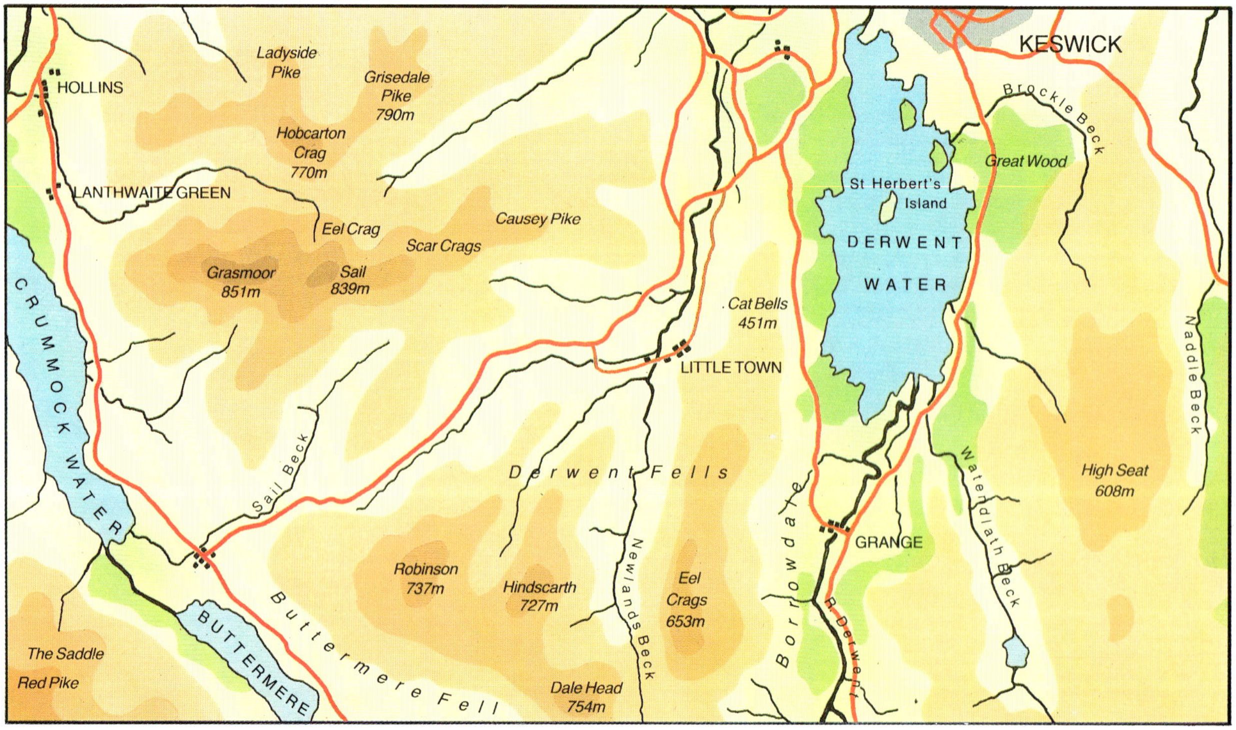

54

4 Pronunciation. Listen to the recording. How many words do you hear in each sentence? What are they? (Contractions like *there's* count as two words.)

5 Look at the town plan. Imagine that somebody asked you how to get from the car park to the post office. What would you say? If you don't know the answer, put these sentences in order.

Then take the first left.
You'll see it on your left.
Then turn right at the first crossroads.
Go straight ahead for about 200 metres.
Keep straight on past the station.

6 Work in groups. Ask and give directions from the car park to other places on the map. Example:

'Excuse me. Can you tell me the way to the Rainbow Theatre?'
'Yes. Go straight ahead...'

7 Can you write down the names of all the rooms in a typical house?

8 Read the advertisement and listen to the recording. How many differences can you find between the two descriptions of the house?

Central York
MAGNIFICENT TOWN RESIDENCE

Four double bedrooms, luxury bathroom, upstairs and downstairs cloakrooms, lounge, dining-room, kitchen/breakfast room, double garage, beautiful mature garden, gas-fired central heating. In first-class condition.

£90,000

Rainbow Theatre

Post Office

Swimming Pool

Railway Station

Town Hall

ANTONIO AVENUE

MAHON STREET

Lennox Way

HIGH STREET

Goldberg Close

STATION ROAD

Police Station

LORD CHANCELLOR'S DRIVE

OSBORNE ROAD

Superb Cinema

Caplan Road

AVENUE

Edward VIII Way

Agricultural College

Sir Percy Shorter Park

Jonah's Way

SHORTER DRIVE

JOYCE

Franklyn Road

JAMES

Car Park

Romainville Hospital

Metres
0   50   100   150   200

9 Work in groups of three or four. Tell the other students in the group about a place that you like. It can be somewhere in the country, a town, a street, a building, or any other kind of place.

10 Listen to the song, and see how much you can understand. Then look at the words on page 156, listen again, and sing along.

B Things

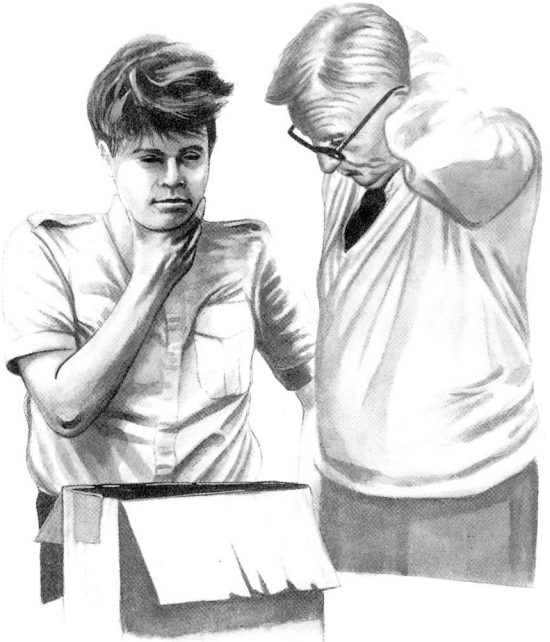

1 Listen to the conversation and learn the new words and expressions.

A: Funny, isn't it?
B: Yes. I didn't think it would be so big.
A: No.
B: Do you like it?
A: I don't know. I'm not sure. Give me time.
B: It looks heavy.
A: Yes, it's quite heavy. Try and pick it up.
B: Ooooh! My back!
A: See?
B: It feels really cold. Like ice.
A: I know.
B: And it smells funny.
A: Sort of sweet.
B: Yes. What's that thing on the top? What's it for?
A: I don't know. Perhaps it's to open the lid with.
B: Fred.
A: Yes, Pete?
B: What *is* it?

2 Put these words and expressions into the sentences.

a bit	feel	funny	isn't it	like	looks
smells	so	sort of	sure	think	with

1. 'Is that Mary?' 'I'm not ....'
2. 'Do you like my hair like this?' 'Not really. I think it looks a bit ....'
3. It was a good film. But I didn't .... it would be .... long.
4. Your sister looks .... you.
5. My brother looks .... like my father.
6. 'The house .... funny.' 'Yes, I've been cooking fish.'
7. I .... funny. .... hot and cold all over.
8. It's cold today, ... ?
9. That baby .... like a football .... arms and legs.

3 Listen to the recording and say what you think the things might be. Begin *It sounds like...* Example:

'It sounds like a train.'

4 What are these?

1. A thing that takes you from place to place.
2. A thing that tells you the time.
3. A thing (that) you read to find out what has happened in the world.
4. A thing (that) you sit on.
5. A thing (that) you open the door with.
6. A thing (that) you drink out of.
7. A small animal with long ears.
8. An animal that has a very long neck.
9. An animal that has black and white stripes.
10. A very big animal with a very long nose.

In sentences 3–6, the word *that* can be left out. In sentences 1 and 2, it can't. Why?

5 How quickly can you match the words and the descriptions?

boat	calendar	envelope	gun	hairbrush
ice-cream	microphone	pillow	suitcase	
tap	tongue	wrist		

1. A thing water comes out of.
2. A thing you tidy your hair with.
3. Something that makes you cool in hot weather.
4. Something you put a letter in.
5. A part of your body that joins your hand to your arm.
6. A thing you can travel in across water.
7. Something you put your head on at night.
8. A thing you speak into.
9. A thing that can kill people.
10. Something that tells you the date.
11. A thing that is useful when you travel.
12. Something you use for talking and tasting.

6 Now describe these.

a nail

a pig

a rose

a magazine

a sheet

a suit

a sandwich

an umbrella

a church

a lipstick

an overcoat

Make up descriptions of some more things. See if the other students can work out what they are.

7 Pronunciation. Say these words and expressions.

1. is it didn't think big thing with lid pick liquid
2. It feels cold. Eat it. What is it? Is it liquid?
3. like time quite alive white mine
4. light high tight might right flight
5. give pint bicycle litre

8 Match the numbers and the pictures.

	LIQUID OR SOLID?	ALIVE?	USEFUL?	CAN YOU EAT/ DRINK IT?	MANUFAC-TURED?	CAN YOU WEAR IT?
1	S	NO	YES	YES	NO	NO
2	L	NO	YES	YES	YES	NO
3	S	YES	YES	NO	NO	NO
4	S	NO	YES	NO	YES	YES
5	S	NO	YES	NO	YES	NO
6	L	NO	YES	NO	YES	NO
7	S	NO	NO	NO	NO	YES

9 Twenty questions.

One student thinks of something. The student doesn't tell the others what it is; he/she only tells them that it is 'animal', 'vegetable', 'mineral' or 'abstract'. (For example: a leather handbag is animal, a newspaper is vegetable, a glass is mineral and an idea is abstract.) The other students must find out what the thing is by asking questions (maximum 20); the only answers allowed are *Yes* and *No*. Useful questions:

Can you eat it?
Is it made of wood/metal/glass?
Is it useful?
Can you find it in a house/shop/car?
Is it liquid?
Is it hard/soft/heavy/light?
Have you got one of these?
Is there one in this room? In this building?
Is it manufactured?

10 Listen to the recording of some people playing 'Twenty questions'.

a sweater

a pint of beer

a pearl

a litre of oil

a bicycle

a cat

a boiled egg

57

Families

A Different kinds of families

1 Match the texts and the pictures. You can use a dictionary.

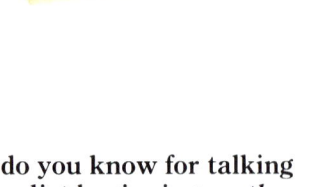

1. Don and Lola are Kenny's grandparents. Kenny has lived with them since he was a baby. Last year they adopted him as their own child.
2. Kim and May are married, but they do not want to have children. Although they enjoy playing with their nieces and nephews, they do not want to be full-time parents.
3. John and Christine have got three children – Simon, Lucy and Emma. There are a lot of couples with young children in their neighbourhood, so they often help one another out.
4. Anamita has got four children. Besides her husband, Surendra, and the children, she also shares her home with her mother-in-law, her brother-in-law and his wife. The children get on well with their aunt and uncle, and like listening to their grandmother's stories.
5. Claire and Bridget live together. They both work outside the home and share the care of Beth, Bridget's six-year-old daughter.
6. Ann has been divorced for ten years. Her two children, Jason and Ruth, live with Ann, and see their father almost every week.
7. Because Jack is too ill to live alone, he lives with his son Barry, who is 25. Barry is getting married soon, and Jack will continue to live with the young couple. He hopes to have grandchildren to look after soon.

2 Pronouncing words together. Some words change their pronunciation before vowels. Listen to the differences in pronunciation.

1. they   they adopted him
2. who   who is 25
3. Claire   Claire and Bridget

Now pronounce these.

4. she also shares
5. too ill to live alone
6. their aunt and uncle
7. Barry is getting married
8. see their father almost every week
9. the care of Beth

3 How many words do you know for talking about relatives? Make a list beginning *mother, father,...* and see how many words you can add.

4 Tell other students about your family or other families you know. Examples:

'My uncle is divorced. His son...'
'My neighbours have got six children. ...'

5 Find these words in the texts in Exercise 1.

also	although	and	because
besides	but	so	

Now put one of the words into each blank in this text.

.... there are many different kinds of families in the world, there are some things that are the same everywhere. Not all societies have western-type marriage with one wife and one husband, ... some kind of marriage is universal. And when a person marries, ... the new wife or husband, he or she also gets a complete new family of in-laws. Marriages with close relatives do not always produce healthy children, ... all societies have rules about who can marry who. Each society .... has a division of work based on age and sex. In modern western societies, there is a move to change this last rule .... it can be unfair to women, ... it will be interesting to see if this succeeds.

6 Class survey. Make sure you understand the questions. Then choose one question to ask the other people in the class.

a. Would you like to live alone part of the time – say, one week a month?
b. Would you rather have more or fewer brothers and sisters than you have?
c. Would you like to have children? How many? OR: Would you like to have more or fewer children than you have?
d. Would you rather live in the same town as your parents or not?
e. Would you rather spend less time working and more time with your family?
f. Would you rather give your parents the money to have a nice holiday on their own, or take them on holiday with you?
g. Would you rather invite your in-laws to spend a week with you, or stay at home while your husband/wife visits them?
h. What's the best age for having children? Is it better to be young or a bit older?

7 Report the results of your survey. Example:

'Nine people would rather spend less time working and more time with their families, and six people think they see enough of their families.'

8 Listen to the recording. Some British people are answering questions from the survey. As you hear their answers, write the letters of the questions they are answering.

9 Listen to the song and try to write down the verbs.

MY OLD DAD

We never .... him in the mornings
And he always .... home late
Then he .... and .... the paper
And .... the crossword while he ....

He never .... us with our homework
But he .... me how to swim
And he .... me to be patient
I guess I .... a lot from him

   My old dad
   He was one of the good guys
   He was nobody's hero
   But he was special to me

Every summer we .... to Blackpool
Except when he .... unemployed
He .... to .... and .... the sunset
That .... one thing we both ....

He .... always very gentle
Nothing ever .... him mad
He .... never rich or famous
But I .... proud of my old dad

   My old dad
   He was one of the good guys
   He was nobody's hero
   But he was special to me

10 Tell other students about someone in your family that you are proud of.

B Family life

Dear God,
Are boys better than girls, I know you are one but try to be fair.

Sylvia.

My mother said she won't get maried again it's too much truble

my mum only likes little babies.when they get old Like me she smacks them.

1 Listen to the conversation.
Can you fill in the missing words?

MIKE: Do you think housewives .... be .... in the same
.... as other people ....? I mean, everybody
.... who does a regular job .... a salary.
SUE: Yeah, but who .... them? That's the trouble. I mean, who
.... they be paid by? The only way you could do it is by
.... the man enough of a wage to pay you as well. And
that, that, er, I mean, in our .... age, in my parents' age
anyway, my .... was paid ...., um, to pay, to support
his wife and .... Nowadays that's not always ....
JOHN: There's no, there's no way you could pay a .... now.
She's doing about ten jobs.

If they don't want you to make your own breakfast. they should say so before

Timmy

2 Listen to the conversation. You will hear
four of the expressions listed below. Which
ones?

the wife stays at home   comes home to work
the end of his day's work
the end of the wife's working day
to work until midnight   If you both share
Well, that's it   I'll pick my feet up
I'll read the newspaper

3 One, two or three stresses? Put the expressions from the box into three lists. Example:

1	2	3
Of course.	*Perhaps you're right.*	

> Of course. Perhaps. Yes, I think so.
> No, I don't agree. I'm not sure. I agree.
> Well, it depends. Probably. Yes, and...
> No, I don't think so. Yes, definitely.
> Of course not. Oh, I don't know.
> Yes, but... Right. Perhaps you're right.

Now put the expressions in order, going from strong agreement to strong disagreement.

4 Work in groups. Each student should choose one of the sentences below, and make sure that all the other group members say what they think about it.

1. Housewives should be paid a salary.
2. Husbands should do some of the housework.
3. Children should do some of the housework.
4. Even young children should get regular pocket money.
5. Children should be free to choose their own friends.
6. When children are 16, they should be free to do what they like.

5 Write a sentence yourself about family life. See if other students agree with it.

6 Turn to the page your teacher tells you. Invent the other half of the dialogue. Write *only* the invented half on a sheet of paper. Then close your book and find a partner to make a complete dialogue with.

mothers and other nasty people frighten children to make them be good

Women do the washing up and clearing and tidying and men go on the train and get tired.

You should never hit a baby because it can't hit back

61

Hopes and wishes

A Would you like to have a white Rolls Royce?

1 Listen to the recording and write down a phrase from the box for each blank.

> I'd like to   I'd like to   I'd like to
> I'd really like to   I'd really like
> I would like to   I *would* like
> I'd love to   I'd just like to

KEITH: .... work in a museum.
JOHN: I think .... own me own gardening centre. I'd love that. (*Yeah*) Yeah. .... that.
SUE: .... be a really good potter. (*Hm-hm. Yeah.*) Be on my own. (*Yeah*)
JANE: .... be really good at something.
ALEX: Actually with the job I've chosen, the police force, ... go into dog handling in that. That's what ....
KATY: I think .... teach again.
MIKE: What .... spend my time doing isn't really classed as jobs.

2 Work in groups. Make some true sentences.

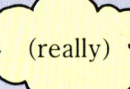

> I'd/I would
> My sister would
> My husband would
> etc.

> (really)

> like to
> love to

> work...
> own...
> be a really good...
> be really good at...
> go into...
> ... again.
> spend my time...

Now close your books and tell some people from other groups what was said in your group. Examples:

'*Michiko would like to go into accounting.*'
'*Kurt's sister would love to own a horse.*'

3 Pronunciation. Listen to the words, and try to pronounce them correctly.

no so go hope know broke spoke over don't won't
open closed Rome phone

Now listen to the definitions, and say which words the speaker is talking about.

Example:

The past of 'speak'. Spoke.

4 Look at the questions and prepare your answers. You can answer as follows:

> '*Yes.*' '*I think so.*' '*I don't think so.*'
> '*I hope so.*' '*I hope not.*' '*I don't know.*'
> '*No.*' '*No, I don't.*' '*No, I won't.*'

When you are ready, close your book, listen to the questions, and answer them.

1. Will you live to be 100 years old?
2. Will you get married next year?
3. Is it going to rain tomorrow?
4. Will everyone come to the next English class?
5. Will you be ill next week?
6. Are there going to be any Olympic Games in the year 2000?
7. Do you hope to travel to America some day?
8. Do you dream in English?
9. What did your teacher want to do when he/she was younger?
10. Will you be very rich one day?
11. Did anyone in your class want to be a doctor when they were younger?
12. Would you like to go to the moon?

5 What did you want to be or do when you were younger? Write three sentences and give them to the teacher. Then try to guess whose sentences the teacher is reading.

> I wanted to be...
> I wanted to study...
> I wanted to...

> but
> and

> my parents wanted me to...
> my teachers wanted me to...
> I changed my mind.
> I still want...
> now I...

6 Choose another member of the class. Write a letter.

Dear ....,
I think you *want to / are going to / hope to / are going to try to* .... *by 1995 / by the end of the year / before you are 80* etc.; and I think
.... Am I right?
Yours,

....

Now answer the letter(s) you have received.
Example:

> Dear Kirsten,
> You are right about one thing
> but wrong about the other.
> I do want to go to Japan,
> but I'm not going to buy a
> sports car.
> Yours,
> Frédérique

7 Class survey. Choose one of the things in the list and ask the other students if they would like it. Examples:

'Would you like to have a white Rolls Royce?'
'Yes, I would.'

'Would you like to be famous?'
'No, I certainly wouldn't.'

to have: more money   a different job   more free time
a better love-life   (more) children   more patience
your picture in a magazine   political power in your country
a different house/flat   more friends   a private plane
a white Rolls Royce   a big motorbike
two wives/husbands

to be: famous   an artist   three years old

to: sleep until midday every day   live to be 100
speak a lot of languages   travel a lot   own a museum

8 Report the results of your survey. Examples:

'Three people out of twelve would like to travel a lot.'
'One person would like to be famous.'
'Everyone would like to speak a lot of languages.'

'Nobody would like to have a yacht.'
'Most people would like to have a private plane.'
'Not many people would like to live to be 100.'

B Could you do me a favour?

1 Complete the two conversations with the words and expressions in the boxes.

PAUL: Hey, John.
JOHN: Yeah?
PAUL: ....?
JOHN: Sure. What is it?
PAUL: Well, ..., I'm
.... until Friday.
......................, do you think?
JOHN: Yes, OK.
PAUL: ...., John. ....
JOHN: ....

> the thing is   Thanks a lot
> Could you do me a favour
> That's all right   short of money
> Could you lend me a fiver
> That's very nice of you

ANNIE: ....
We've got a problem.
MR OLIVER: Oh yes? ....?
ANNIE: Well, ...,
.... We're cycling, and
we haven't got ....
tonight.
MR OLIVER: ....
the Crown Hotel?
ANNIE: Yes. It's .... too
expensive. So .... sleep
in your barn.
MR OLIVER: Yes, ...
.... You don't smoke,
do you?
ANNIE: Oh, no. Neither of us do. Well,
....
MR OLIVER: ....
come into the house for a wash?
ANNIE: ....
MR OLIVER: ....

2 Can you find some examples of informal and formal language in the two conversations?

INFORMAL	FORMAL
Hey	Excuse me.
Yeah?	Oh, yes?
. . .	. . .

> Have you tried   much   all right   you see
> Excuse me   Not at all   Would you like to
> thank you very much   I don't mind
> This way   I'm sorry to trouble you
> What's the matter
> I see   we wondered if we could
> it's like this   anywhere to sleep
> That's very kind of you

3 Practise the conversations with a partner.

4 Look at the pictures. In each picture, somebody wants somebody else to do something.
(i) Which pictures go with sentences 1–4?   (ii) Listen to the four spoken sentences.
Which pictures go with them?   (iii) Make sentences yourself for the last four pictures.

1. He wants them to sign a petition.
2. They want him to give them some water.
3. He wants her to take the dog for a walk.
4. He wants his father to lend him his car.

5 Pronunciation. Listen to the recording and write the words and expressions that you hear.

6 Work in pairs or groups of three. Make up a conversation for one of the pictures. Use some of the words and expressions from the conversations in Exercise 1.

Money

A Where does all the money go?

1 How much (approximately) is £1 in your currency? How much is £10? £50? $1? $20? $100? Make a note and try to remember. Then complete the table by guessing an amount for each blank. Listen to the recording and check your answers.

AVERAGE BRITISH HOUSEHOLD EXPENDITURE 1983

(Pounds per week after taxes and insurance)

Housing	£24.62
Fuel, electricity	7.24
Food	
Alcoholic drink	10.14
Tobacco	
Recreation, entertainment, education	13.03
Clothing, footwear	
Household goods and services	10.14
Other goods and services	17.38
Transport and communication	

2 Look at the table in Exercise 1 and answer the questions as quickly as you can.

1. What did the average family spend most on in 1983?
2. Which of the things in the table did they spend least on?
3. True or false? They spent more on alcohol than on heating and electricity.
4. Did they spend more on food than on housing?
5. Did they spend less on clothing than on transport and communication?
6. True or false? They spent nearly twice as much on alcohol as on tobacco.
7. True or false? Alcohol and tobacco together cost more than half as much as housing.

3 Say what you think about the figures in Exercise 1. Does the average British family spend too much on some things and not enough on others, in your opinion?

4 Make some sentences about your own expenditure this year, last year and next year. Examples:

'This year I've spent a lot of money on...'
        I've spent too much on...'
        I haven't spent much on...'

'Last year I spent a lot on...'
        I spent too much on...'
        I didn't spend much on...'

'This year I've spent less/more on... than last year.'

'Last year I spent less/more on... than this year.'

'I must spend less on... next year.'
'I can spend more on... next year.'

5 Budgets. Alice Calloway is a 25-year-old sales manager. She earns quite a good salary (you decide how much), and lives alone in a small flat. Work with another student and make a budget for Alice. You must decide how much she spends every week (in pounds or dollars) on the following items (you can add more if you want to).

rent
electricity and gas
food and household
travel
books
telephone

clothing and shoes
alcohol
cigarettes
entertainment
miscellaneous
savings

6 Cutting down expenditure. Alice has had to change her job for personal reasons. Her income is now 25% lower than it was. Exchange budgets with another pair of students. Your job now is to cut down Alice's expenditure by 25%. When you have done this, explain your changes to the two students who made the budget. Examples:

'We think Alice spends too much on...'
'She must spend less on...'
'She must travel less.'

67

B I'll give you £25 for it

1 Listen to the conversation. Learn the new words and expressions. Then close your book, listen again, and try to write down the missing words.

A: How much do you want for it?
B: Forty.
A: Forty pounds?
B: Yes. It's worth fifty, but I'm in a hurry.
A: I don't know. It's not in very good condition. Look. This is broken. And look at this. I don't think it's worth forty. I'll give you twenty-five pounds.
B: Twenty-five? Come on. I'll tell you what – I'll take thirty-five. Since you're a friend of mine. You can have it for thirty-five.
A: No, that's still too much. To tell you the truth, I can't afford thirty-five.
B: I'm sorry. Thirty-five. That's my last word.
A: Come on, let's split the difference. Thirty pounds.
B: Thirty. Oh, very well. All right, thirty.
A: Can I give you a cheque?
B: Well, I'd prefer cash, if you don't mind.

2 Say these sentences from the dialogue. Remember to link the marked words.

How much do you want for it?
I'm in a hurry.
I don't know.
I don't think it's worth forty.
Since you're a friend of mine.
You can have it for thirty-five.
Come on, let's split the difference.
Can I give you a cheque?
Well, I'd prefer cash, if you don't mind.

3 Work with a partner. Each of you tries to sell something to the other, and you try to agree on a price. But you can't buy or sell until each of you has used at least two of the words or expressions you wrote down in Exercise 1.

4 Grammar revision. Put *too*, *too much* or *too many* in each blank.

1. 'How much are the carrots?' 'Forty pence a pound.' 'That's ....'
2. She doesn't go skiing any more. She's .... old.
3. You're driving .... fast. Please slow down.
4. If you eat .... chocolate, you'll get fat.
5. I've got .... books – I don't know where to put them all.
6. You've given me .... meat. I can't eat it all.

5 *Enough, not . . . enough* or *too*? Example:

1. *too short* OR *not tall enough*.

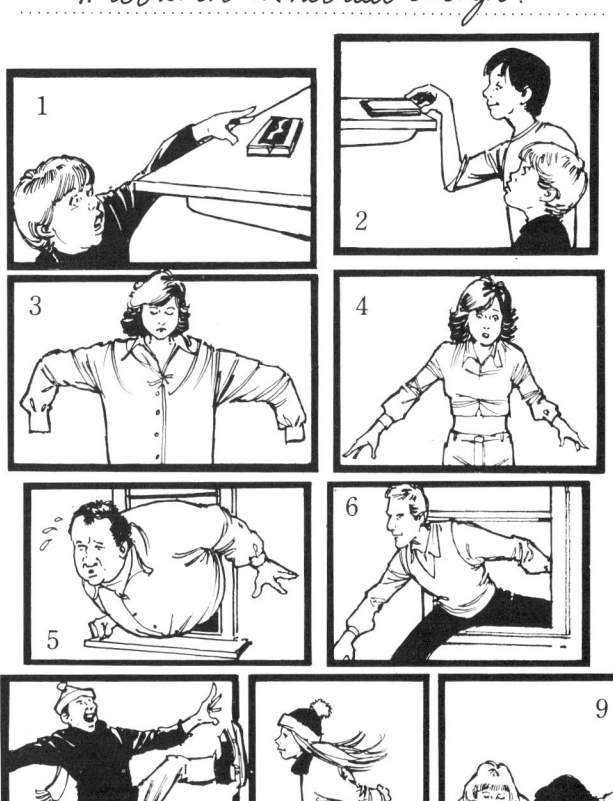

6 Copy the list of names; then listen to the recording of an auction. How much did each person pay?

Hunt   Holtby   Crowther   Day   Drew

Here is a list of some of the items sold at the auction. Listen again and match the items to the names of the people who bought them. There are some extra items.

a. Cigarette box, lighter and ashtray
b. Two boxes of miscellaneous
c. Espresso coffee maker
d. Blue and white bowl and cover
e. White chest of four drawers
f. Portable lights in excellent condition
g. Small bedroom chair

7 Ian and David have just rented a flat. They are going to an auction to buy some furniture. But they can't find anything they want. Match the sentences below with some of the lettered objects in the picture.

1. It's too heavy to carry.
2. It's too long to fit in the living room.
3. It's not big enough to hold all my books.
4. It's not strong enough to put anything on.
5. It's too difficult to clean.

Now imagine why Ian and David aren't buying some of the other things in the picture. Write two sentences with *too...* and two sentences with *not... enough*.

69

Before and after

A Do you get up as soon as you wake up?

1 Choose one of these questions (or make up a similar question) and ask as many people as possible. Make a note of the answers.

1. Do you get up as soon as you wake up?
2. Do you have breakfast before or after you get dressed?
3. Do you put your left shoe on before your right?
4. Do you make the bed before or after you have breakfast?
5. Do you undress before you brush your teeth at night?
6. Do you put the light out before or after you get into bed?
7. Do you go to bed at a fixed time, or do you wait until you're tired?
8. Before you go to sleep, do you usually read in bed?
9. Do you pay bills as soon as you get them?
10. Before you buy something, do you always ask the price?
11. Do you put salt on food before or after you taste it?
12. Do you read the newspaper before or after you arrive at work?
13. Do you address an envelope before or after you close it up?
14. Do you answer letters as soon as you get them?
15. Do you wait until your hair is too long before you go to the hairdresser?
16. Do you have to translate English sentences before you can understand them?
17. What are you going to do after the lesson has finished?
18. Are you going to study English before you go to bed tonight?
19. Will you study any more languages after you have learnt English?
20. Will you keep on working until you're 60?

2 Report the answers to the class.
Examples:

*'Four students out of twelve have breakfast before
    they get dressed.'*
*'Sixty per cent of the students read the newspaper
    after they arrive at work.'*
'Most people put their left shoe on before their right.'

3 How do you usually spend the evening?
Write a paragraph using this skeleton.

When I ...., I .... Then
I .... and .... After that
I .... Then I .... until
.... Before I ...., I
....

4 Pronunciation. Say these words.

1. possible   on   long   not   stop   want
2. before   more   report   always   salt
   saw   course   caught   bought
3. note   go   envelope   close   coat

**Now put these words into groups 1, 2 or 3.
(One word does not belong in any of the
groups.)**

no   off   short   got   home   other   fall
thought   draw   lost   horse   open   boat
gone   don't

**Can you find any more words to put in the
three groups?**

5 Look at picture 1 and study the examples. Then put *still*, *yet* or *already* into the sentences.

1

John's still in bed.
He hasn't got up yet.
Susan is already dressed.

The postman has .... been.
Jane hasn't picked up her letters ....
They are .... on the mat.

Alice's taxi is .... waiting in front of her house.
Alice isn't ready ....
She is .... in the bath.

'Have you had lunch ....?'
'No, I'm .... working. What about you?'
'I've .... eaten.'

Peter and Ann are both 19.
Ann is .... at school.
Peter is .... married.
He hasn't got any children ....

Jake is nearly 40, but he .... plays football every Saturday.
His son Andy is not 15 ...., but he is .... a good footballer, too.

6 Listen to the conversation between a commercial traveller and his boss. The traveller has to visit five places: Birmingham, Coventry, Dudley, Leamington and Wolverhampton (not in that order). Can you list the towns in the order in which he has visited them or will visit them?

7 Read the story.

ALISON BOGLE

Chapter 1
Alison Bogle lived in Exeter and worked in a bookshop. She was 23 – slim and pretty, rather shy and very quiet. She spent most of her spare time reading; at the weekend she went walking on the moors, or drove over to see her parents in Taunton.

Alison was quite happy, but sometimes she wished she didn't have such a quiet life. Exeter was not really a very exciting place. At half past ten at night, all the lights went out. Nobody ever danced in the streets – at least, Alison had never seen it happen. And it rained all the time. *All* the time.

There were so many things Alison would like to do. So many things she hadn't done. For example, she had never been in an aeroplane.

Chapter 2
....
....
....

Chapter 3
Alison poured herself another glass of champagne and smiled at Carlos. What a man! He was so handsome. And such a good dancer. And so kind to her. Alison had never met anybody like him. She wondered what he was thinking.

The sun, shining down through the palm trees, made a moving pattern of light and shade on the sand. Carlos smiled back at her and stood up. He took her hand. 'Come on, let's have another swim,' he said.

8 Work with two or three other students. Make up Chapter 2 of the story. Then tell your Chapter 2 to another group.

B I hadn't seen her for a very long time

1 Choose the correct words and expressions to put in the gaps.

I .... down the street one day   *walked / was walking*
Looking at the shops
When someone asked me if I .... the way.   *know / knew*
I gave the girl directions
And then saw who it was.
I couldn't .... of anything to say.   *think / to think*

I hadn't seen her .... a very long time   *since / for*
Since the day we said goodbye.
She .... changed,   *hasn't / hadn't*
She .... looked young and shy.   *still / yet*
I thought perhaps .... changed so much   *I / I'd*
She didn't .... it was me,   *realise / realised*
Then I saw the recognition in her eye.

We stood in silence for a while,
Then I led her to a bar.
I felt as if I .... with a ghost.   *was walking / had walked*
We drank and began to talk
And then her eyes met mine.
Her eyes .... always shown her feelings most.   *have / had*

We .... about the good old days   *talked / have talked*
About family and friends
About the hopes we'd shared .... it all went   *before / after*
  wrong.
She seemed quite pleased to see me
So I .... two more drinks,   *ordered / had ordered*
But when I got back to the table she .... gone.   *has / had*

I hadn't seen her for a very long time *etc.*

2 Listen to the song and check your answers.

3 Past perfect tense. Look at the examples and then do the exercise.

PAST (THEN):	I **saw** who it was.
EARLIER PAST (BEFORE THEN):	I **hadn't seen** her for a very long time.
PAST:	We **talked** about...
EARLIER PAST:	...the hopes we**'d shared.**

Put in the correct tense (simple past or past perfect).

1. When we .... talking, I realised that we .... before. (*start; meet*)
2. When I .... at my suitcase, I could see that somebody .... to open it. (*look; try*)
3. When we got to the restaurant, we found that nobody .... to reserve a table. (*remember*)
4. The doctor ....him, and found that he .... his arm. (*examine; break*)
5. Before my 18th birthday I .... out of England. (*not be*)
6. We were a few minutes late, so the film .... when we .... to the cinema. (*already start; get*)
7. When she got to England, she found that the language was quite different from the English that she .... at school. (*learn*)
8. 'Good afternoon. Can I help you?' 'Yes. I .... my watch to you for repair three weeks ago. Is it ready yet?' (*bring*)

4 Pronunciation. Listen to the recording. How many words do you hear in each sentence? What are they? (Contractions like *I'd* count as two words.)

5 Listen to the story and then put the pictures in the right order.

6 Can you talk about one of these?

1. A day in your life when everything went wrong.
2. A meeting with somebody that you hadn't seen for a very long time.

Facts and opinions

A They thought the sun went round the earth

1 What did people believe hundreds of years ago?
Make sentences.

'They used to think that . . .'

the sun	was flat
the sky	could be made into gold
the earth	were born from mud
heavy things	was the centre of intelligence
lead	was made of crystal
the heart	went round the earth
insects	fell faster than light things

Do you know any other strange things that people used to believe?
Did you believe any strange things when you were a child?

2 Who found out what?

Pasteur proved that
Fleming found out that
Harvey showed that
Darwin said that
Newton proved that
Lucretius believed that

light
everything
people
penicillin
the blood
illnesses

were caused by very small living creatures.
was made up of colours.
circulated round the body.
was made up of atoms.
would kill bacteria.
were related to monkeys.

Can you think of other things that famous scientists have found out?

3 Pronunciation. Say these sentences with the correct stress.

1. People **thought** that the **earth** was **flat**.
2. They be**lieved** that the **sky** was **solid**.
3. They **thought** that the **sun** went **round** the **earth**.

Where are the stresses in these sentences? Can you say them?

4. They thought that the stars were holes in the sky.
5. They didn't know that the sun was a star.
6. They believed that mountains were the homes of gods.

4 Change the quotations from direct speech to reported speech. Examples:

Marx: 'Religion is the opium of the people'.
Marx said that religion was the opium of the people.
The young George Washington: 'I cannot tell a lie'.
Washington said that he could not tell a lie.

1. Stevenson: 'To travel hopefully is better than to arrive'.
2. Dorothy Parker (of another woman): 'She speaks 18 languages, and she can't say "no" in any of them'.
3. Somebody (of President Gerald Ford): 'He can't walk and chew gum at the same time'.
4. Anita Loos: 'Gentlemen prefer blondes'.
5. Oscar Wilde: 'It is better to be beautiful than to be good'.
6. The British Prime Minister Harold Wilson: 'A week is a long time in politics'.
7. Calderon: 'Life is a dream'.
8. *The Daily Express* in 1938: 'There will be no war in Europe'.
9. Dr Dionysus Lardner (1793–1859): 'Rail travel at high speed is impossible because people will not be able to breathe'.
10. Professor J.H. Pepper: 'The electric light has no future'.
11. Simon Newcomb, American astronomer: 'Artificial flight is impossible'.
12. Professor Tait: 'The telephone is physically impossible'.
13. Admiral Leahy, US Navy, June 1945: 'The atom bomb will never go off, and I speak as an expert in explosives'.

5 Listen to the recording and try to complete the sentences. The words in the box will help you.

> light   right   ring   satellite   speed
> telescope   true   wrong

1. The ancient Greek philosopher Aristotle said that heavy things fell...
2. For 2,000 years everybody believed that Aristotle...
3. In the 16th century, scientists started to wonder if Aristotle's beliefs...
4. The Italian scientist Galileo did some experiments which proved that Aristotle...
5. He showed that heavy things...
6. Galileo was the first person to...
7. He found out that Jupiter...
8. and that Saturn...
9. and that there were mountains...
10. and spots...

6 Work in groups of about four. Prepare some 'general knowledge' questions to ask other students. Begin *Do you know...?* or *Can you tell me...?* Examples:

'Do you know if gold is heavier than lead?'
'Can you tell me whether Britain has a king or a queen?'
'Do you know what his or her name is?'
'Do you know who Marco Polo was?'
'Can you tell me who Robert Redford is?'
'Do you know where the President was born?'
'Can you tell me who discovered radium?'
'Do you know who invented the telephone?'
'Do you know where Toronto is?'

B Probability

1 Look at the information about Fred Smith. Then listen to the recording of a conversation between Fred and a girl at a party. What did he say that was not true? Example:

'Fred said that he lived in Paris and California.'
'He told the girl that he had been to Venice.'

FRED SMITH
Full name: Frederick George Smith.
Age: 25
Address: 17 Victoria Terrace, Highbury, London N5.
Profession: van driver.
Interests: photography, model aeroplanes.
Education: Finsbury Park Comprehensive School.
Qualifications: none
Father: Albert Eric Smith, 52, shop assistant.
Mother: Florence Anne Smith, née Henderson, 48, housewife.

2 Here are some of the things that Fred said in the conversation. Do you think they are true? Use one of the expressions in the box.

It must be true.	It's probably true.
It could be true.	It might be true.
It's probably not true.	It can't be true.

1. My friends call me Fred.
2. I photograph famous people.
3. I travel all over the world.
4. I've been photographing the President for *Time* magazine.
5. Famous people are all the same.
6. I find you interesting.
7. I want to photograph you.
8. I love poetry.

LLANDYFRDWY

3 Look at the picture. What can you say about the time and place? Examples:

'It might be morning, because...'
'It can't be in Germany, because...'
'It must be during the day, because...'

4 Pronunciation. Say these words.

1. star   stop   stand   studio   start   student
2. speak   spoke   Spain   spend
3. score   Scotland   Scottish
4. spring   spread   strange   street   straight
   screw   scratch   scream

5 Look at the examples to see how *likely* is used.

She **is likely to** come soon. = She **will probably** come soon.
I **am likely to** need help. = I **will probably** need help.

Now express these ideas using *likely.*

1. I will probably go to Spain soon.
2. She will probably spend next week in London.
3. It will probably stop raining soon.
4. You will probably meet some strange people at John's house.
5. If you start learning English now, you will probably speak it quite well by next summer.
6. They say the spring will probably be wet this year.

Now look at these examples.

There is likely to be a phone call for me.
   = **There will probably be** a phone call for me.
There are likely to be about 20 people at the party. = **There will probably be** about 20 people at the party.

Now express these ideas using *there is/are likely to be...*

1. There will probably be an election in June.
2. There will probably be some problems.
3. There will probably be snow in Scotland.
4. There will probably be a parking place in this street.

6 What is likely to happen in your life? In your country? In the world? Make sentences with *likely.*

7 Reading and dictionary use.

1. **Read the text and write down the words you don't know. Do *not* use a dictionary.**
2. **Read the text again. How well can you understand it? (*Very well/quite well/not very well/not at all.*)**
3. **Look at the words you wrote down. Have you got any idea what some of them mean? Look at the text and see if you can guess.**
4. **Which of the words do you really need to look up in a dictionary, to understand the text well? Look them up and read the text once more.**
5. **Choose some of the new words to learn.**

THE AMAZON FOREST AND THE FUTURE OF THE WORLD

The Amazon forest, in Brazil, covers five million square kilometres – an area as big as the whole of Europe excluding Russia. It contains one third of the world's trees.

However, the trees are disappearing. By 1974, a quarter of the forest had already been cut down. In the following year, 1975, 4% of the remaining trees went. If the destruction of the forest continues at the same rate, there will be nothing left by the year 2005.

Scientists say that the disappearance of the trees is already causing changes in the climate. In Peru, there is less snow than before on the high peaks of the Andes mountains. In Bolivia, there is less rain than before and more wind. In some parts of north-east Brazil there is now very little rain.

What will happen if more of the Amazon forest is cut down? According to climatologists, two things are likely to happen: there will be serious effects on the world's climate, and the air that we breathe will lose some of its oxygen. Why is this?

Trees absorb the gas carbon dioxide from the air, and give out oxygen into the air. The trees of the Amazon rain forest are chemically very active, and some scientists believe that they provide 50% of the world's annual production of oxygen. If we lose the tropical forests, the air will contain much less oxygen and much more carbon dioxide. It will become difficult – perhaps even impossible – to breathe.

With more carbon dioxide in the air, the temperature will rise; the ice-caps at the North and South Poles will melt; the sea level will rise, and hundreds of coastal cities will be flooded.

Scientists do not all agree about the exact figures – the calculations can be done in different ways with different results. But all scientists agree that if we destroy the Amazon forest it will be environmental suicide – like losing an ocean. Life on earth will become difficult, and it may become impossible.

Small talk

A Hello, nice to see you

1 Listen to Dialogue 1, and write the numbers and letters of the expressions you hear.

1. A I go.
   B I'm going.
   C I'll go.

2. A Nice to see you.
   B It's nice to see you.
   C Nice seeing you.

3. A Are we late?
   B We're late.
   C Aren't we late?

4. A You're first
   B You're the first
   C You're not first

5. A Who is coming?
   B Who ever's coming?
   C Who else is coming?

6. A Can I take your coat?
   B Let me take your coat.
   C Shall I take your coat?

7. A You know Lucy, do you?
   B You know Lucy, don't you?
   C You don't know Lucy, do you?

8. A I think we've met her once.
   B I think we met her once.
   C I think we'll meet her one day.

9. A What can I get you to drink?
   B What can I give you to drink?
   C What would you like to drink?

10. A The room doesn't look nice, John.
    B The room does look nice, John.
    C Doesn't the room look nice, John?

11. A You've changed it about
    B You've changed it round
    C You've changed it over

2 Listen again. Which of these do you hear?

A don't you?   D wasn't it?
B do you?   E aren't we?
C isn't it?   F haven't you?

3 Real questions or not? Listen to the sentences. Does the voice go up or down at the end? Examples:

The piano was over by the window, wasn't it?
You know Lucy, don't you?

1. It's a lovely day, isn't it?
2. You're French, aren't you?
3. She's got fatter, hasn't she?
4. The train leaves at 4.13, doesn't it?
5. Children always like cartoon films, don't they?
6. It's your birthday next week, isn't it?
7. Hotels are expensive here, aren't they?
8. Ann said she'd phone, didn't she?

4 Work with two or three other students. Act out a 'greeting' scene like the one in Dialogue 1.

5 Listen to Dialogue 2. Then look at the following sentences. Are they true or false? Write 'T' (true), 'F' (false), or 'DK' (don't know).

1. Lucy works in a pub.
2. She likes her work.
3. She doesn't meet many interesting people.
4. Lucy's job is always hard work.
5. There is only one barman in her pub.
6. John works in a bank.
7. He likes his job very much.
8. He has just been made manager.
9. He's going to move to another town soon.
10. Lucy wouldn't like to move to another town.
11. John has lived in the same place for six years.

6 Listen again. Can you remember some sentences from the dialogue?

7 Real questions. Listen and repeat.

1. That's hard work, isn't it?
2. You're an accountant, aren't you?
3. You have to move round, don't you?
4. It'll be in another town, won't it?

8 Asking for agreement. Listen and repeat.

1. It's a nice day, isn't it?
2. She's very pretty, isn't she?
3. Good clothes are expensive, aren't they?
4. You're tired, aren't you?

9 Work with four or five other students. You are all in the same compartment on a long train journey. Act out a conversation in which you get to know one another.

10 Listen to Dialogue 3. Write down all the words you hear for things that you can eat or drink.

11 Can you complete these questions from the dialogue?

What are you looking ....?
What are John and Lucy talking ....?

Now read the following answers and write the questions.

1. They're talking about politics.
   What are they talking about?
2. I went with Henry.
3. I'm looking for Alice.
4. I bought it for you.
5. I'm thinking about holidays.
6. I'm listening to some piano music.
7. I'm looking at your ear-rings.
8. The letter was from Andy.

12 Asking for agreement. Listen, and say the 'question-tags'. Example:

It's a nice day, ...

... isn't it?

79

B I didn't think much of it

2 Which of these words and expressions come in the dialogue?
Write down your answers; then listen again and see if you were
right.

I liked it all   lovely   nonsense   I didn't think much of it
I cried   I couldn't help it   It made him laugh
It didn't say anything to me   I may be very old-fashioned
So am I   I like violence   Why did you like it?
It was really really boring   three old men   Who wrote it?
I've never heard of him

1 Listen to Dialogue 4.
What do you think they were
talking about?
Can you remember any of the
things they said?

3 Write down the names of a food, a sport,
an animal and a person (singer, actor,
writer, ...) that you like. Tell another student,
and listen to his or her answers.

I like ...
I quite like ...
I really like ...
I like ... very much.
I love ...

So do I.
I don't.
I quite like him/her/
it/them.
I've never heard of
him/her/it/them.

Write down the names of a food, a sport, an
animal and a person (singer, actor, writer, ...)
that you don't like.
Tell another student and listen to his or her
answers.

I don't like ...
I don't much like ...
I really don't like ...
I don't like ... at all.

Neither do I.
I do.
I don't mind him/her/
it/them.
I've never heard of
him/her/it/them.

80

4 Write down the names of three books/films/plays etc. that you liked and three that you didn't.
Tell other students and listen to their answers.

> I liked...
> I really liked...
> etc.

> So did I.
> I didn't.
> I didn't think much of it.
> I haven't seen it.
> I've never heard of it.
> etc.

> I didn't like...
> I didn't much like...
> etc.

> Neither did I.
> I did.
> I quite liked it.
> I haven't read it.
> etc.

5 Talk some more about books/plays/films etc. that you have read or seen.

6 Listen to Dialogue 5. The following sentences are like sentences in the dialogue, but they are not exactly the same.
What are the exact sentences in the dialogue?

It's late.
We've got to go a long way.
We'd better go, too.
Thank you very much, Ann.
I really enjoyed myself.
Thanks for coming.
You must come and see us soon.
I'll phone you.
This isn't mine.
Well, who is this, then?
It's old and dirty.

7 Look at the dialogue texts on pages 156–158.
Choose a sentence and try to say it with a good pronunciation.
The teacher will say it for you correctly.

8 Listen to Dialogues 1–5 again.
Read the texts, and write down some useful expressions to learn.

9 Improvisation. Work in groups of six to eight. Act out a dinner party. How long can you go on for?

Do it

A How to do it

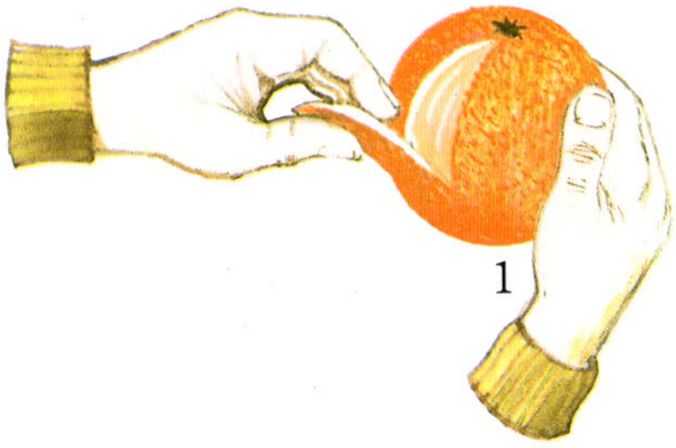

1 **Match the words and the pictures.**

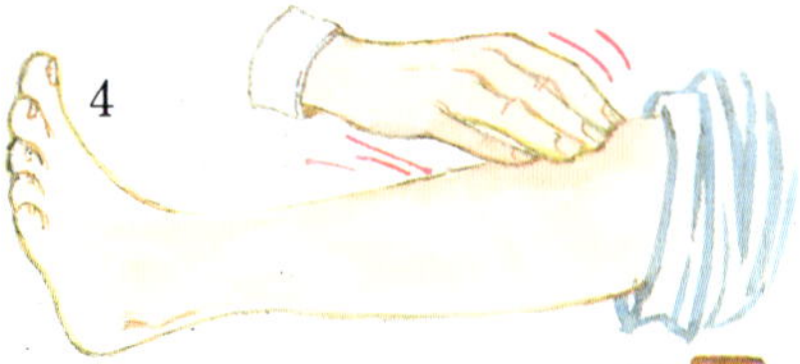

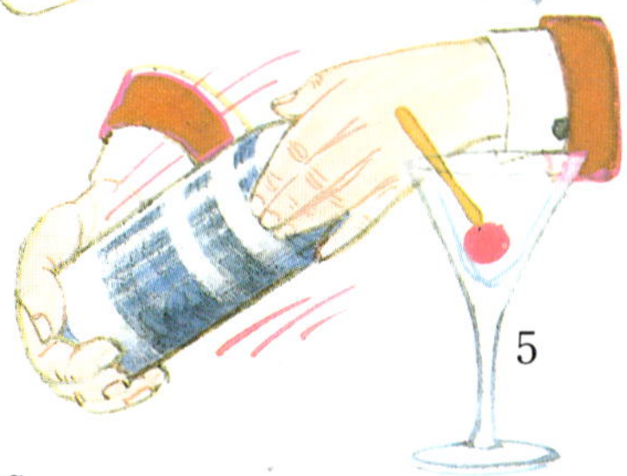

cover	peel	rub
scratch	shake	stick

2 Here are some useful practical tips for everyday life. Unfortunately, the beginnings and ends have got mixed up. Can you sort them out?

To make tomatoes easier to peel,
If you want to pick up a rabbit,
To get cigarette stains off your fingers,

If you catch German measles,

You can clean dirty saucepans

To get dust out of a guitar,
If two glasses are stuck together,

To get small scratches off your watch glass,
You can make tight shoes more comfortable

rub them with lemon first and then wash them.
rub it with liquid brass cleaner.
cover them with very hot water for a minute or two.
put cold water in one and stand the other in hot water.
by packing them with wet newspaper and leaving them overnight.
don't hold its ears.
don't visit anyone who is pregnant unless you're sure she's already had them.
put rice inside it, shake it and empty it.
by filling them with cold water and vinegar and letting them boil for five minutes.

3 How do you think these tips begin?

... don't put your address on the outside of your luggage.
... by rubbing it with a cut potato or apple.
... put a glass of beer a few yards away.
... hold the back over the steam from a kettle.

4 Can you complete these tips?

The night before an examination, ...
To find out how far away a thunderstorm is, ...
You can get a tight ring off by ...

5 Work in groups. Each group writes four tips (serious or funny ones). Then copy the tips, with the beginnings and ends out of order, and give them to another group to put in order.

6 Say these words. Notice the stress.

1. side   ex**ci**ting   said   ex**cept**
2. pen   spend   ex**pen**sive   speak   ex**pe**rience   sport   **ex**port
3. rest   press   ex**pre**ssion
4. late   play   ex**plain**
5. shave   change   ex**change**

7 Imagine your plane has just crashed on an island where no one lives. You may not be rescued for months. Talk about what there is to do. Examples:

'We'd better build a place to sleep in.'
'We should make a fire that planes can see.'

8 Work with six or seven other students. Make a plan for the class's life on the island. Decide who should do what part of the work and why, and report to the class. Examples:

'We think Giovanna should plan the houses, because she's an architect.'
'Ahmed had better not do any hard work, because he's been ill.'

B If I were you,...

1 Match the expressions and the pictures.

| back to front | face downwards | inside out |
| sideways | underneath | upside down |

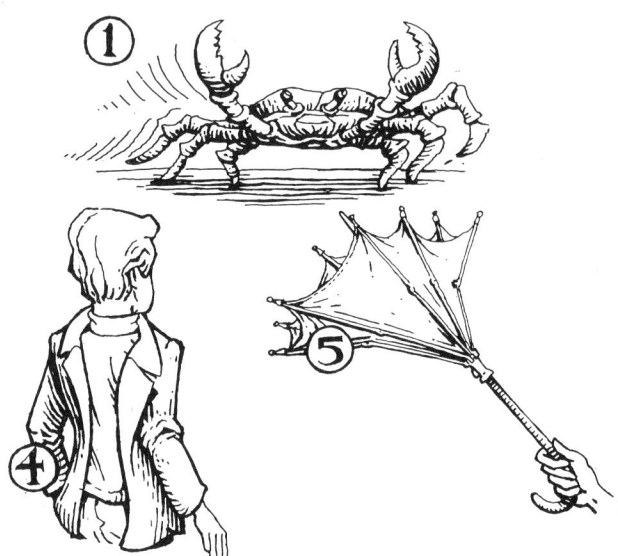

2 Listen to the dialogue. Are there any differences between the version on the recording and the version in the book?

A: If I were you, I'd turn it the other way round.
B: Well, I think I'll try it this way first.
A: I mean, –
C: Hello. I wouldn't do it like that if I were you.
B: Wouldn't you?
C: No, I think you ought to turn it upside down.
B: Oh, really? I'll think about it.
C: Yes, and put a blanket underneath first, or it'll get dirty.
D: Hi. Why don't you turn it sideways?
B: You think so?
D: Oh, yes, and remember to cover it, or it'll get wet.
B: Get wet?
A: You really ought to take the wheels off first, you know.
B: Well, I –
E: I think it would be much better if he turned it back to front, don't you?
A: That's just what I said.
D: Don't forget to tighten all the screws up.
C: You're not getting anywhere like that.
D: If I were you, I'd go back to the beginning and start again.
C: And I still think you should turn it upside down.
E: Let's help him.
B: It's quite all right. I can do it by myself, thank you very much.
E: No, it's no trouble.
A: Come on, everybody.

3 Look through the dialogue and write down some useful expressions and structures to learn.
Exchange lists with one or more other students and see if you have thought of the same expressions.

4 Fluency practice. Choose a sentence from the dialogue and practise saying it. Try for accurate intonation and rhythm.

5 Put a verb from the box into each blank (or set of blanks). Use some verbs more than once; use the correct tenses.

| be | change | do | explain | have | know |
| look | make | read | ring | stop | take |

A: I don't know what to do. If John *were* here, he ....
B: Yeah, if John .... here, he .... what to do, but .... he .... how to do it? If I .... you, I' .... the instructions again.
A: I've read them twice already. Do you think it .... a good idea if I .... the top off and .... inside?
B: I don't know. I don't think I' .... that if it .... mine.
A: Wouldn't you? What .... you .... if you .... this mess in your kitchen?
B: I' .... worrying about it for the moment; I' .... Pat and .... the problem; I' .... my plans for this evening.
A: Yeah, I suppose you're right. If I .... the top off, I' .... probably just .... it worse. Pour me a drink while I ring Pat, will you?

84

6 Four friends wrote to Christine asking for advice. Here are bits of their letters and bits of her answers. Match the problem to the answer.
Then work in groups: imagine one of the situations and invent the rest of Christine's letter. Try to use some of the expressions you have learnt in this lesson.

has ever been in trouble with the law before

the only time I've been interested in another man, and it's finished now. Should I tell Steve or

parents just don't understand. Just because he's younger than me, they think

must be drugs. She won't talk to us about it, and we don't know who to

you, I would go to the family doctor immediately

were you, I wouldn't say anything to him. I've known him since long before you were married,

as bad as it seems. If you can't afford a good lawyer, she ought to be able to get one free by

Why don't I talk to your mother? Perhaps her feelings wouldn't get in the way so much if I spoke to her

7 Pronunciation. Say these words.

1. ask   asks
2. ghost   ghosts   post   posts
3. find   finds   mend   mends   sound   sounds
4. tap   taps   envelope   envelopes
5. bank   banks   drink   drinks
6. aunt   aunts   invent   invents
7. tap   tapped   hope   hoped   help   helped
8. like   liked   work   worked   sack   sacked
9. isn't   doesn't   wasn't   hasn't
10. hadn't   wouldn't   couldn't   shouldn't

8 Prepare a short speech (maximum two minutes). In your speech, you must try to make other students do something. For example: stop studying English; leave the room; give up smoking; become vegetarians; change their religion; give you a lot of money; buy you a car; change their jobs.

85

Technology

A Electricity

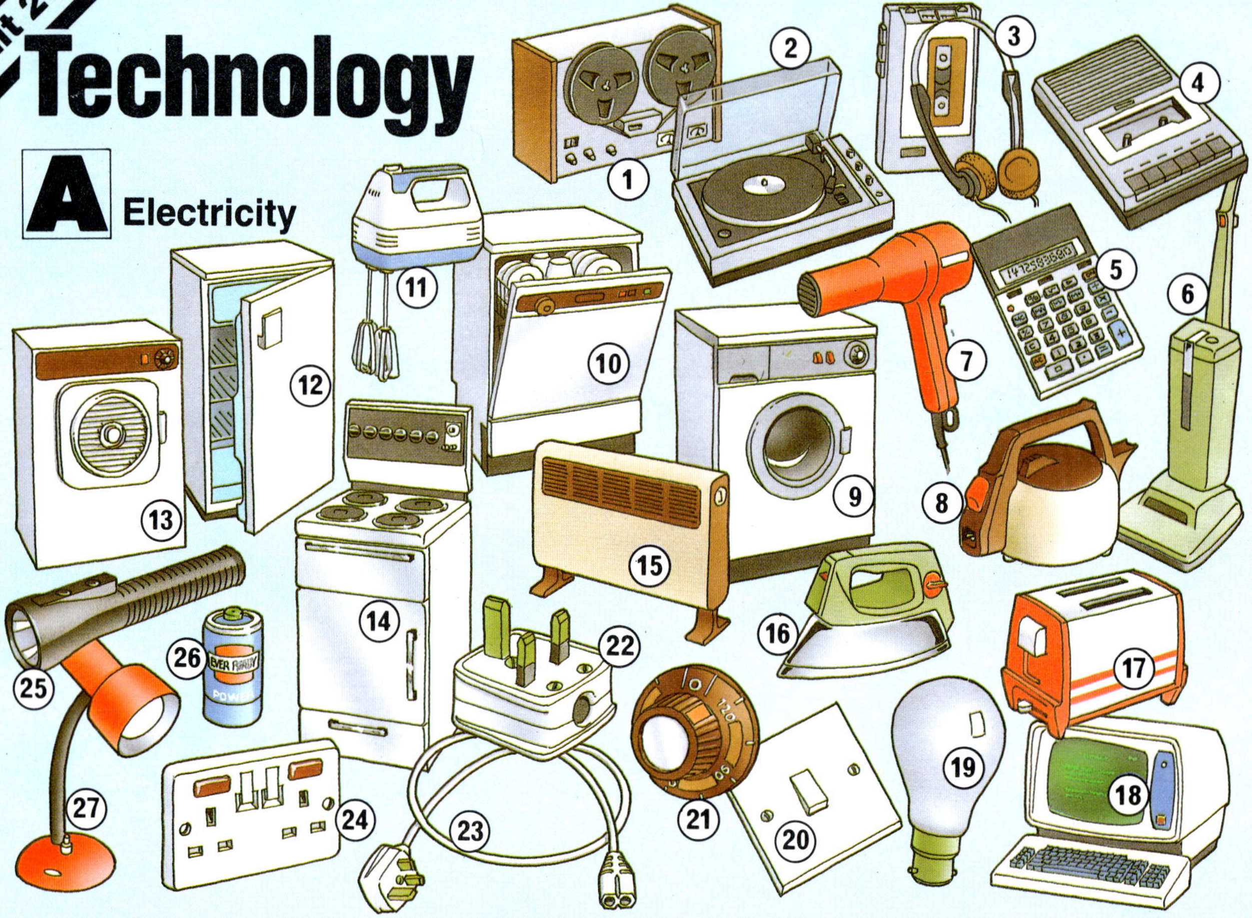

1 Look at the pictures. Do you know the names of some of these things? Work in groups of three or four and try to list as many as possible.

2 In all of these words, the last syllable is pronounced /ə/. Look at the spellings. Then say the words after the recording or your teacher.

heater cooker computer calculator
transistor mirror similar sugar
centre theatre departure figure
there here where hear wear hair
their Africa cinema idea visa

3 If you could have just five of the things in the picture (plus leads, plugs and sockets), which would you choose? Which five are the least important?

4 Which of the things in the picture can you see now? Which of them are somewhere else in the building?

5 Look at the pictures below and listen to the recording. Which thing is described in each sentence? Example:

It's plugged in and switched on. It's black and white.

The radio.

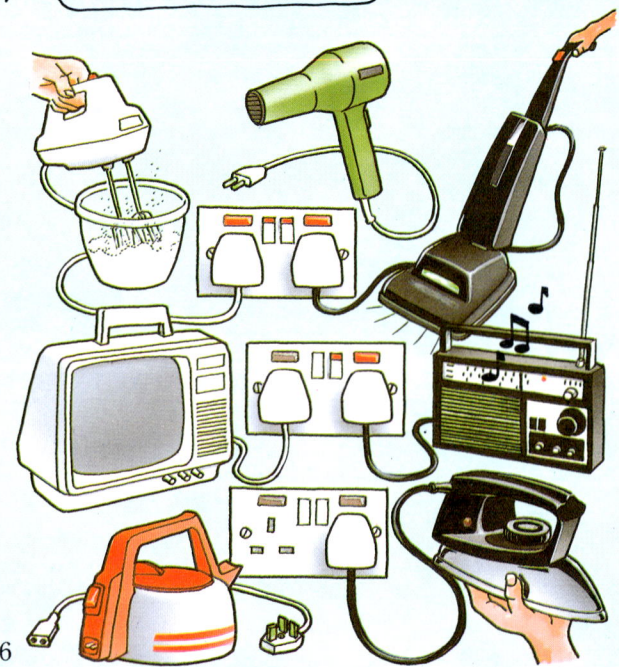

6 Look at the sentences and say what you should do. Use these verbs.

> switch on   switch off   turn up
> turn down   plug in   unplug

Example:

What should you do if you've finished using your calculator? *'Switch it off.'*

What should you do if:
1. the radio isn't loud enough?
2. the record player's too loud?
3. you see in the newspaper that there's an interesting TV programme just starting?
4. you don't want to watch TV any more?
5. the TV's on fire?
6. the cooker's too hot?
7. you want to use your calculator?
8. the iron isn't getting the creases out of your clothes?
9. the iron's burning your clothes?
10. you've finished with the iron?

8 Look at the information and then answer these questions.
1. **How much would your use of electricity cost you every week if you paid British prices?**
2. **Which electrical appliance do people in the class spend the most money on?**
3. **Who spends the most on electricity?**

7 Put in *should, shouldn't, must* or *mustn't.*

1. You .... always switch electrical appliances off when you are not using them.
2. Small children .... watch violent programmes on TV.
3. In Britain, before you start using a new electrical appliance, you .... put the right kind of plug on.
4. When you put a plug on, you .... be careful to put the wires in the right places.
5. You .... touch electrical appliances when you are in the bath.
6. When you move into a new house or flat, you .... check the electrical wiring.
7. You .... plug too many things into the same socket.
8. You .... wash white and coloured clothes separately.
9. You .... clean out the fridge from time to time.
10. You .... let the iron get too hot if you are ironing silk.
11. You .... turn your radio up loud at night.
12. In Britain, you .... buy a licence every year if you have a TV.

THE COST OF ELECTRICITY
1. Electricity is sold by the 'unit'. (You use one unit if you use 1 kilowatt [1,000 watts] of electricity for one hour, or 500 watts for 2 hours, or 100 watts for 10 hours.)
2. In Britain in 1984, one unit cost about 5p.
3. To see what you get for one unit, look at the information below.

WHAT YOU GET FOR ONE UNIT
electric blanket: 2 nights
convector heater: ½ hour
food mixer: over 60 cakes
hair dryer: 3 hours
iron: over 2 hours
kettle: 12 pints of water (7 litres)
light (100w bulb or 1,500mm tube): 10 hours
radio: 20 hours
record player: over 24 hours
fridge: 1 day

clothes dryer (tumble dryer): ½ hour
stereo: 8–10 hours
tape recorder: over 24 hours
black and white TV: 9 hours
colour TV: 6 hours
toaster: 70 slices of toast
vacuum cleaner: 2–4 hours cleaning
electric razor: 2,000 shaves.
hot water: 1 bath, 4 showers or 10 bowls of washing-up water

LARGER APPLIANCES
cooker: it takes 20–25 units to cook one week's meals for a family of four.
dishwasher: one full load uses 2½ units.
freezer: ½ unit per 10 litres per week.
washing machine: it takes 9 units to do the weekly wash for a family of four.

B It doesn't work

1 Match the objects with the problems. You can use a dictionary. The first two answers are done for you.

a. It makes a funny noise. *2,4,7,9*
b. It won't start. *4,7*
c. It won't wind on.
d. It doesn't work.
e. The dial's broken.
f. It won't record.
g. It's started going very fast.
h. It won't stop dripping.
i. One of the buttons is stuck.
j. It won't turn off.
k. I can't hear anything.
l. It smells funny.
m. There's no colour.
n. It keeps flooding.
o. There's something wrong with the engine.
p. It won't ring.
q. It's stopped.
r. It's leaking.
s. The rewind's stuck.
t. It's slow.
u. The flash won't work properly.
v. It keeps sticking.

2 Put in an infinitive or an *-ing* form.

1. My watch has stopped .... (*work*)
2. I would like .... a better stereo. (*buy*)
3. I very much enjoy .... photos of animals. (*take*)
4. Do you like .... sport on TV? (*watch*)
5. I must ask Harry .... my cassette player. (*mend*)
6. We hope .... a new car soon. (*get*)
7. I don't want .... Judy – will you do it? (*telephone*)
8. Our dishwasher keeps .... (*flood*)
9. Thanks very much for .... my bicycle. (*mend*)
10. Don't forget .... some oil in the car. (*put*)
11. I can't stand .... advertisements on TV. (*watch*)
12. We must .... the mixer back to the shop – it doesn't work. (*take*)

3 Listen to the recording. How many words do you hear in each sentence? What are they? (Contractions like *What's* count as two words.)

4 Look these words up in a dictionary or ask your teacher what they mean.

> guarantee   pressure   pressure cooker
> receipt   release   stainless steel

Now listen to the telephone conversation and answer these questions.

1. Is the pressure cooker stainless steel?
2. Is it automatic?
3. What's the problem?
4. Is it under guarantee?
5. Can the man find the guarantee papers?
6. Does the man have the receipt?
7. What is the man's name?
8. Where does the man live: East Hagby, East Hadley or East Hagbourne?
9. Does the woman think she can help him?
10. How long has he had the pressure cooker?
11. What make is it?
12. About how much did the pressure cooker cost?

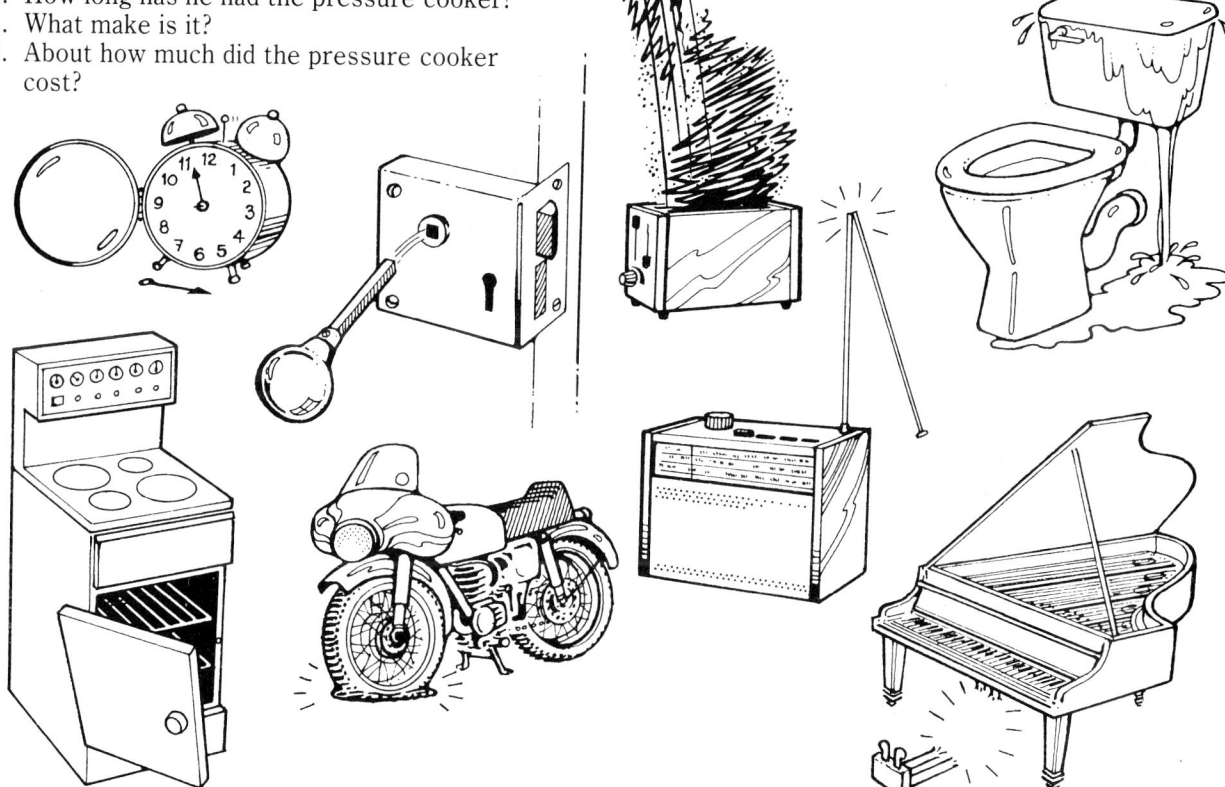

5 Work with a partner, and make up a conversation about something that has gone wrong. You can talk about one of the things in Exercise 1, about one of the things in the pictures on this page, or about something else if you prefer.
Use some of the expressions from Exercise 1, and some of these expressions from the telephone conversation.

Can I help you?
I hope so.
I've got a problem with...
How long have you had it?

What make is it?
Is it under guarantee?
I'll take your name.
Thank you very much for your help.

Revision and fluency practice

A A choice of activities

> Look at the exercises in this lesson. Try to decide
> which of them are most useful for you, and do one
> or more.

LISTENING

1 Listen to the recording. You will hear
some sentences with mistakes in. Answer by
saying the correct sentences (below) with the
right stress. Examples:

'You lost a briefcase, didn't you?'
*'No, I **found** a briefcase.'*

'Sally found a briefcase, didn't she?'
*'No, **I** found a briefcase.'*

'You found a handbag, didn't you?'
*'No, I found a **briefcase**.'*

1. No, I found a briefcase.
2. No, my mother lives in London.
3. No, it's John's birthday on Tuesday.
4. No, I'm a teacher of German and Arabic.
5. No, I live at 37 Edinburgh Road.

2 Listen to the football results and answer
the questions.

1. Did Manchester City win?
2. Who lost against Swansea?
3. How many goals did Manchester United score?
4. What was the score between Liverpool and
   Arsenal?
5. Did Nottingham Forest play at home or away?
6. How many draws were there?

3 Try to fill in the missing words. Then
listen to the song and see if you were right.

A BIGGER HEART

His arms are stronger than mine
His legs are .... than mine
His car's always cleaner
And his grass is always ....

But my heart is .... than his
And my love for you is stronger than his.

His shirts are .... than mine
His soufflés are lighter than mine
His video is ....
And his faults are fewer

But my heart is .... than his
And my love for you is stronger than his.

He's more ...., much more elegant
More charming and polite than me
He's more responsible, much more dependable
He's everything I long to be.

His office is .... than mine
His martinis are drier than mine
His roses are ....
And his overdraft is smaller

But my heart is .... than his
And my love for you is stronger than his.

SPELLING AND PRONUNCIATION

4 Do you know how to pronounce these
words?

Two syllables, not three: asp(i)rin, bus(i)ness,
cam(e)ra, diff(e)rent, ev(e)ning, ev(e)ry,
marri(a)ge, med(i)cine.

Three syllables, not four: comf(or)table,
secret(a)ry, temp(e)rature, veg(e)table, usu(a)lly.

Silent letters: shou(l)d, cou(l)d, wou(l)d, ca(l)m,
wa(l)k, ta(l)k, ha(l)f, i(r)on, i(s)land, lis(t)en, (w)rite,
(w)rong, (k)now, (k)nife, (k)nee, (k)nock, (k)nob,
dau(gh)ter, hei(gh)t, li(gh)t, mi(gh)t, ri(gh)t,
ti(gh)t, strai(gh)t, throu(gh), wei(gh), nei(gh)bour,
ou(gh)t, thou(gh)t, g(u)ess, g(u)ide, g(u)itar,
(h)our, (h)onest, We(d)n(e)sday, san(d)wich,
si(g)n.

**(For a more complete list of spelling and
pronunciation problems, see the Summary.)**

SPEAKING

5 Question-box. Take a question out of the box, read it aloud and answer it. Say at least one sentence; if you like, you can say more. If you don't like a question, you can say *I'd rather not answer*, but you must take another question and answer it.

6 The *yes/no* game. Work in groups. One person has to answer questions for one minute; the others ask him or her as many questions as possible. The person who answers must not say *yes* or *no*.

READING

7 Use your dictionary and get rich. Look at the paper and the map, and try to decide where the money is buried. You can look up *four* words (maximum) in your dictionary. Which four words will you look up?

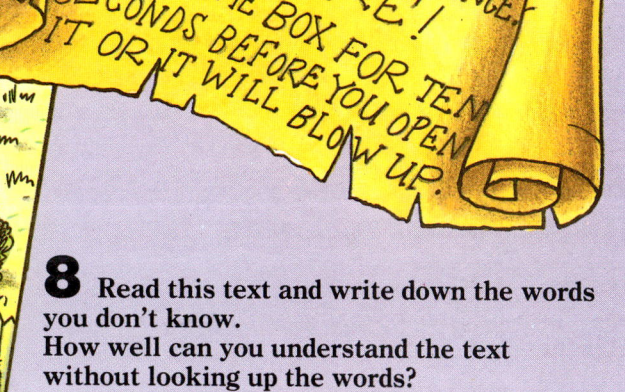

THE MONEY IS CONCEALED IN A BOX IN A HOLLOW TREE. THE TREE IS HALF A FURLONG NORTH-EAST OF THE LARGE BEEHIVE BY THE SOUTH FENCE. BEWARE! JIGGLE THE BOX FOR TEN SECONDS BEFORE YOU OPEN IT OR IT WILL BLOW UP.

8 Read this text and write down the words you don't know.
How well can you understand the text without looking up the words?
Can you guess what any of the words mean?
How many of the words do you *have* to look up?
Look them up and read the text again.

BLACKBEARD'S TREASURE

In the 17th century Spanish ships sailed regularly to Central and South America to fetch gold for the Spanish government. The ships were often attacked by pirates, who infested the 'Spanish Main' (the sea area north-east of Central and South America).

As the pirates could obviously not bank their stolen gold, they buried it. A famous pirate called Blackbeard, who operated on the Spanish Main from 1690 to 1710, hid his treasure somewhere on the coast of North Carolina. He then killed everyone who knew where the treasure was, and boasted 'Only the Devil and myself know the hiding place'.

Perhaps the Devil told somebody, because it seems likely that Blackbeard's treasure was dug up on Christmas Day 1928, at a place called Plum Point in North Carolina. But the gold disappeared again at once: nobody knows who found it, or where it has gone.

91

B What do you say when you...?

1 Here are some pairs of sentences. In each pair, the two sentences mean the same, but one is more formal than the other. Can you divide them into formal and informal?

Hello. .... *F*

Hi. .... *I*

How's it going?
How are you?

Can't complain.
Very well, thank you.

Goodbye.
See you.

Hey!
Excuse me.

Have you got a fiver?
Could you lend me five pounds?

Thank you very much.
Thanks a lot.

Do you mind if I smoke?
Is it OK if I smoke?

How much is that?
What do you want for that?

2 Can you match the expressions and the situations?
Example:

'Can I look round?' Shop

EXPRESSIONS	SITUATIONS
Can I look round?	Shop
I'll put you through.	Doctor's surgery
Fill up with four-star, please.	Lost property office
A single for two nights.	Thanking somebody
Single to Manchester.	Making an appointment
Check in at 9.30.	On the telephone
Second on the left.	Pub
It was green, with a red handle.	Hotel reception
That's very kind of you.	Complaining about faulty goods
I'll give you twenty-five for it.	Garage / petrol station
Pint of bitter, please.	Bank
It won't switch off.	Replying to thanks
Could we make it a bit later?	Hairdresser
How would you like it?	Airport
It hurts when I bend down.	Giving directions
Not at all.	Bargaining
Not too short, please.	Station

92

3 Choose five of the situations and see if you can think of another typical expression for each one.

4 Work with two or three other students. Make a list of typical expressions for one of the situations. Your teacher will help you.
Useful questions:

How do you say . . . ?
What do you say when . . . ?
What's the English for . . . ?
How do you pronounce . . . ?
How do you spell . . . ?
What does . . . mean?

5 Prepare and practise a conversation for the situation which you studied in Exercise 4.

93

Unit 12: Lesson A

Grammar and structures

Simple present passive

Trees **are transported** to paper mills
    by land or water.
(= Somebody transports trees to
    paper mills...)

Made from and *made into*

Paper **is made from** wood. Wood **is
    made into** paper.

No *the* in generalisations

Paper was invented by the Chinese.
Oil is produced in Texas.
    (**NOT** ~~The oil is produced...~~)

Words and expressions to learn

industry /ˈɪndəstri/
page /peɪdʒ/
adult /ˈædʌlt/
dry /draɪ/
use /juːz/
grow (grew, grown)
    /grəʊ, gruː, grəʊn)/
reach /riːtʃ/
get to /ˈget tə/
AD /eɪ ˈdiː/
by land /baɪ ˈlænd/
daily /ˈdeɪli/
serious /ˈsɪərɪəs/
Muslim /ˈmʌzlɪm/

Learn five or more of these:
rice /raɪs/
oil /ɔɪl/
coal /kəʊl/
wheat /wiːt/
wool /wʊl/
gold /gəʊld/
chemicals /ˈkemɪkʊlz/
iron /ˈaɪən/
steel /stiːl/
plastic /ˈplæstɪk/
leather /ˈleðə(r)/
cotton /ˈkɒtn/
synthetic fibre /sɪnˈθetɪk ˈfaɪbə(r)/
produce (verb) /prəˈdjuːs/
mine /maɪn/
manufacture /mænjʊˈfæktʃə(r)/
invent /ɪnˈvent/

Unit 12: Lesson B

Grammar and structures

Simple past passive

All three **were arrested** the next morning.
The *Communist Manifesto* **was written** by Marx and Engels.
  (**NOT** ~~. . . was writing by. . .~~)

With and *by*

He was killed **with** a revolver.
  (= Someone used a revolver to kill him.)
The police think he was killed **by** his wife.
  (= The police think his wife killed him.)
His leg was broken **by** the fall.
  (**NOT** ~~. . . with the fall. . .~~)

Words and expressions to learn

stone /stəʊn/
dance /dɑːns/
body (= dead person) /'bɒdi/
thief /θiːf/
business /'bɪznɪs/
invent /ɪn'vent/
direct /dɪ'rekt/
arrest /ə'rest/
sack /sæk/
owe /əʊ/
search /sɜːtʃ/
import /'ɪmpɔːt/
export /'ekspɔːt/
alive /ə'laɪv/
central /'sentrʊl/
earlier /'ɜːlɪə(r)/

Revision vocabulary: do you know these words?

pocket /'pɒkɪt/
cash /kæʃ/
hotel /həʊ'tel/
flat /flæt/
discover /dɪs'kʌvə(r)/
kill /kɪl/
build (built, built) /bɪld (bɪlt)/
win (won, won) /wɪn (wʌn)/
dead /ded/

Unit 13: Lesson A

Words and expressions to learn

hill /hɪl/
valley /'væli/
stream /striːm/
waterfall /'wɔːtəfɔːl/
wood /wʊd/
path /pɑːθ/
lake /leɪk/
town hall /'taʊn 'hɔːl/
college /'kɒlɪdʒ/
park /pɑːk/
central heating /'sentrʊl 'hiːtɪŋ/

through /θruː/
straight ahead /'streɪt ə'hed/

Revision vocabulary: do you know these words?

across /ə'krɒs/
along /ə'lɒŋ/
up /ʌp/
down /daʊn/
north /nɔːθ/
south /saʊθ/
west /west/
east /iːst/
mountain /'maʊntɪn/
island /'aɪlənd/

river /'rɪvə(r)/
bridge /brɪdʒ/
road /rəʊd/
town /taʊn/
car park /'kɑː 'pɑːk/
post office /'pəʊst 'ɒfɪs/
crossroads /'krɒsrəʊdz/
theatre /'θɪətə(r)/
cinema /'sɪnəmə/
street /striːt/

Unit 13: Lesson B

Grammar and structures

Linking verbs with adjectives

It **looks heavy**.
  (**NOT** ~~It looks heavily.~~)
It **is heavy**.
It **feels cold**.
It **smells funny**.

Look like, sound like etc.

Your sister **looks like** you.
It **sounds like** a train.

That: relative pronoun

a thing **that** tells you the time
an animal **that** has a very long neck

a thing (that) you sit on
something (that) you read

Prepositions at the end of relative clauses

a thing (that) you sit **on**
a thing (that) you open the door **with**
a thing (that) you drink **out of**

With

an animal **with** a long neck
  (= an animal **that has** a long neck)

You (= people)

A watch tells **you** the time.
A key is a thing that **you** open the door with.

Words and expressions to learn

back /bæk/
ice /aɪs/
tongue /tʌŋ/
envelope /'envələʊp/
feel (felt, felt) /fiːl (felt)/
smell (smelt, smelt) /smel (smelt)/
funny (= strange) /'fʌni/

Learn seven or more of these:
lid /lɪd/
calendar /'kælɪndə(r)/
suitcase /'suːtkeɪs/
hairbrush /'heəbrʌʃ/
pillow /'pɪləʊ/
sheet /ʃiːt/
wrist /rɪst/
queue /kjuː/
sandwich /'sænwɪdʒ/
microphone /'maɪkrəfəʊn/
lipstick /'lɪpstɪk/
magazine /mægə'ziːn/
nail /neɪl/
overcoat /'əʊvəkəʊt/
rose /rəʊz/
umbrella /ʌm'brelə/
beer /bɪə(r)/
litre /'liːtə(r)/
oil /ɔɪl/
pig /pɪg/

Revision vocabulary: do you know these words?

top /tɒp/
boat /bəʊt/
gun /gʌn/
ice-cream /'aɪs 'kriːm/
tap /tæp/
church /tʃɜːtʃ/
suit /suːt/
bicycle /'baɪsɪkl/
pint /paɪnt/
sweater /'swetə(r)/
cat /kæt/
sure /ʃɔː(r)/
heavy /'hevi/
pick up /'pɪk 'ʌp/
wear (wore, worn) /weə(r) (wɔː(r), wɔːn)/
liquid /'lɪkwɪd/
alive /ə'laɪv/
useful /'juːsfʊl/
a bit /ə 'bɪt/

Unit 14: Lesson A

Grammar and structures

Would rather

Would you **rather** live in the same town as your parents or not?
(**NOT** ~~Would you rather to live...~~)
I'd rather take my mother on holiday with me.
I'd rather not invite my in-laws to spend a week with us.
Most people **would rather** spend less time working.

Connectors

Kim and May are married, **but** they do not want to have children.
Although they enjoy playing with their nieces and nephews, they
   do not want to be full-time parents.
There are a lot of couples with young children in their
   neighbourhood, **so** they often help one another out.
Besides her husband and her children, she **also** shares her home
   with her mother-in-law, ...
Because Jack is too ill to live alone, he lives with his son Barry.
Barry is getting married soon, **and** Jack will continue to live with
   the young couple.

Words and expressions to learn

relative /'relətɪv/
aunt /ɑ:nt/
uncle /'ʌŋkl/
niece /ni:s/
nephew /'nefju:/
cousin /'kʌzn/
grandmother /'grænmʌðə(r)/
grandfather /'grænfɑ:ðə(r)/
granddaughter /'grændɔ:tə(r)/
grandson /'grænsʌn/
mother-in-law /'mʌðərɪnlɔ:/
father-in-law /'fɑ:ðərɪnlɔ:/
brother-in-law /'brʌðərɪnlɔ:/
sister-in-law /'sɪstərɪnlɔ:/
parents-in-law
   /'peərəntsɪnlɔ:/
in-laws /'ɪnlɔ:z/
society /sə'saɪəti/
rule /ru:l/
adopt /ə'dɒpt/
continue /kən'tɪnju:/
universal /ju:nɪ'vɜ:sl/
healthy /'helθi/
proud (of) /praud (əv)/
although /ɔ:l'ðəu/
besides /bɪ'saɪdz/

Revision vocabulary: do you know these words?

parent /'peərənt/
child (*plural* children) /tʃaɪld ('tʃɪldrən)/
grandparent /'grænpeərənt/
grandchild /'græntʃaɪld/
husband /'hʌzbənd/
wife (*plural* wives) /waɪf (waɪvz)/
daughter /'dɔ:tə(r)/
son /sʌn/

Unit 14: Lesson B

Grammar and structures

Should

Husbands **should do** some of the housework.
   (**NOT** ~~Husbands should to do...~~)

Words and expressions to learn

housewife /'hauswaɪf/
wage /weɪdʒ/
housework /'hauswɜ:k/
support /sə'pɔ:t/
own /əun/
regular /'regjulə(r)/
upset /ʌp'set/
special /'speʃl/
free /fri:/
nowadays /'nauədeɪz/
pocket money /'pɒkɪt 'mʌni/
(fifteen)-year-old
   /(fɪf'ti:n) jɪər 'əuld/
You're right. /jɔ: 'raɪt/

Revision vocabulary: do you know these words?

midnight /'mɪdnaɪt/
foot (*plural* feet) /fut (fi:t)/
school /sku:l/
disco /'dɪskəu/
end /end/
pay /peɪ/
stay /steɪ/
agree /ə'gri:/
think (thought, thought) /θɪŋk (θɔ:t)/
choose (chose, chosen) /tʃu:z (tʃəuz, 'tʃəuzn)/
enough /ɪ'nʌf/
true /tru:/
early /'ɜ:li/
late /leɪt/
of course /əv 'kɔ:s/
perhaps /pə'hæps/
it depends /ɪt dɪ'pendz/
definitely /'defənətli/

Unit 15: Lesson A

Grammar and structures

Would like

Would you **like** to have a white Rolls Royce?
   No, I **wouldn't**. / Yes, I **would**.
I'd like to be very rich.
Everybody **would like** to speak a lot of languages.

Want

I **wanted to study** Spanish, but my teachers **wanted me to study** Latin.
   (**NOT** ~~... my teachers wanted that I study...~~)

Other ways of expressing wishes and hopes

I'm going to try to learn another language before I'm 30.
I hope to finish paying for my car by the end of the year.

By

I'll be there **by** three o'clock. (=at or before three,
   but not later)

Words and expressions to learn

museum /mju:'zi:əm/
the moon /ðə 'mu:n/
Japan /dʒə'pæn/
magazine /mægə'zi:n/
patience /'peɪʃəns/
artist /'ɑ:tɪst/
midday /mɪd'deɪ/
own (verb) /əun/
good at /'gud ət/
open (adjective) /'əupn/
different (= other) /'dɪfrənt/
political /pə'lɪtɪkl/
really /'rɪəli/
again (=as before) /ə'gen/
everyone /'evriwʌn/
by (with time expressions) /baɪ/

145

Unit 15: Lesson B

Grammar and structures

Want + object + infinitive
They **want him to give** them some water.
   (**NOT** ~~They want that he gives them...~~)

Wondered if + past tense
We **wondered** if we **could** sleep in your barn.
I **wondered** if you **were** free.

Words and expressions to learn

favour /'feɪvə(r)/
Could you do me a favour?
letter /'letə(r)/
post (verb) /pəʊst/
Sure (of course) /ʃɔ:(r)/
well, ... /wel/
the thing is, ... /ðə 'θɪŋ 'ɪz/
Thanks a lot.

short of money
That's all right.
you see, ... /ju: 'si:/
it's like this
We wondered if we could...
Not at all. /nɒt ət 'ɔ:l/
this way

Unit 16: Lesson A

Grammar and structures

Quantities
They spend **too much** on tobacco.
They don't spend **enough** on food.
They spent **less** on clothing than on transport.
They spent **more** on food than on housing.
How much is £6 in your currency?
I've spent **a lot of** money on clothes.
   (**NOT** ~~I've spent much money...~~)
I haven't spent **much** on furniture.
I spent **a lot** on transport last year.
   (**NOT** ~~I spent much on...~~)
She must travel **less**.

Saying amounts of money
£5.25 = 'five pounds and twenty-five pence' or
'five (pounds) twenty-five'

No article with general meanings
They spent a lot on **food**. (**NOT** ~~...on the food.~~)
Alcohol and **tobacco** together cost less than half
   as much as housing.
   (**NOT** ~~The alcohol and the tobacco...~~)

Must and *can*
Alice **must** spend less on clothing.
   (**NOT** ~~Alice must to spend...~~)
We **can** spend more on entertainment next year.
   (**NOT** ~~We can to spend...~~)

Use of verb tenses with time expressions
This year I've spent a lot of money on...
Last year I spent a lot on...
Next year I must spend less on...
Next year I can spend more on...

Words and expressions to learn

electricity /ɪlek'trɪsəti/
goods /gʊdz/
transport /'trænspɔ:t/
opinion /ə'pɪnjən/
currency /'kʌrənsi/
budget /'bʌdʒɪt/
rent /rent/
savings /'seɪvɪŋz/
income /'ɪnkʌm/
earn /ɜ:n/
spend (spent, spent) /spend (spent)/
miscellaneous /mɪsə'leɪnɪəs/
personal /'pɜ:sənʊl/
exchange rate /ɪks'tʃeɪndʒ 'reɪt/

Learn three or more of these:
fuel /'fju:əl/
tobacco /tə'bækəʊ/
clothing /'kləʊðɪŋ/
services /'sɜ:vɪsɪz/
alcohol /'ælkəhɒl/
communication /kəmju:nɪ'keɪʃn/

Unit 16: Lesson B

Grammar and structures

Making proposals
I'll give you twenty-five pounds.
I'll tell you what.

Quantifiers
If you eat **too much** chocolate, you'll get fat.
I've got **too many** books – I don't know where
   to put them all.
'You can have it for thirty-five.' 'No, that's still
   too much.'

Too... and *not...enough*
It's **too** heavy to carry.
It's **not** big **enough** to hold all my books.

Words and expressions to learn

pound (weight) /paʊnd/
cover /'kʌvə(r)/
drawer /drɔ:(r)/
chest of drawers /'tʃest əv 'drɔ:z/
portable /'pɔ:təbl/
worth /wɜ:θ/
since (=because) /sɪns/
a friend of mine /ə 'frend əv 'maɪn/
can('t) afford /kn ('kɑ:nt) ə'fɔ:d/
in...condition /ɪn... kən'dɪʃn/
Come on. /'kʌm 'ɒn/
I'll tell you what. /aɪl 'tel ju: 'wɒt/
To tell you the truth, ... /tə 'tel ju: ðə 'tru:θ/
Oh, very well. /'əʊ 'veri 'wel/
I'd prefer... /aɪd prɪ'fɜ:(r)/
if you don't mind /ɪf ju: 'dəʊnt 'maɪnd/

Revision vocabulary: do you know these words?

old /əʊld/
fat /fæt/
heavy /'hevi/
strong /strɒŋ/
difficult /'dɪfɪkʊlt/
long /lɒŋ/
small /smɔ:l/

Unit 17: Lesson A

Grammar and structures

Time clauses
I usually read for a bit **before I go to sleep**.
Before I go to sleep, I usually read for a bit.
I enjoyed life more **after I left school**.
After I left school, I enjoyed life more.
Give John my love **when you see him**.
When you see John, give him my love.
I'll phone you **as soon as I arrive**.
   (**NOT** ~~as soon as I will arrive.~~)
As soon as I arrive, I'll phone you.
I'll wait **until you're ready**.

Still, yet and already
John's **still** in bed.
He hasn't got up **yet**.
Susan is **already** dressed.

So and such
so handsome
such a handsome man
so quiet
such a quiet life
so kind to her
such a kind person
so good
such good bread
so happy
such happy people

Words and expressions to learn

postman /'pəʊstmən/
mat /mæt/
commercial traveller /kə'mɜːʃl 'trævlə(r)/
make a bed /'meɪk ə 'bed/
undress /ʌn'dres/
brush one's teeth /'brʌʃ wʌnz 'tiːθ/
put out (a light) (put, put) /'pʊt 'aʊt/
go to bed (went, gone) /'gəʊ tə 'bed (went, gɒn)/
address (a letter) /ə'dres/
answer (a letter) /'ɑːnsə(r)/
translate /trænz'leɪt/
keep on (kept, kept) (...ing) /'kiːp 'ɒn (kept)/
report /rɪ'pɔːt/
as many as possible /əz 'meni əz 'pɒsəbl/

Unit 17: Lesson B

Grammar and structures

Past perfect tense

I had (I'd) gone
you had (you'd) gone
he/she/it had (he'd/she'd/it'd) gone
we had (we'd) gone
they had (they'd) gone

had I gone?
had you gone?
had he/she/it gone?
had we gone?
had they gone?

I had not (hadn't) gone
you had not (hadn't) gone
he/she/it had not (hadn't) gone
we had not (hadn't) gone
they had not (hadn't) gone

Simple past and past perfect

PAST (THEN):   I **saw** who it was

EARLIER PAST
(BEFORE THEN):   I **hadn't seen** her for a
   very long time

PAST: We **talked** about...

EARLIER PAST: ...the hopes we**'d shared**.

Words and expressions to learn

the way (to somewhere) /ðə 'weɪ/
directions /də'rekʃənz/
recognition /rekəg'nɪʃn/
silence /'saɪləns/
ghost /gəʊst/
feelings /'fiːlɪŋz/
the good old days /ðə 'gʊd 'əʊld 'deɪz/
hope /həʊp/
meeting /'miːtɪŋ/
look /lʊk/
realise /'rɪəlaɪz/
lead (led, led) /liːd (led)/
go wrong (went, gone) /'gəʊ 'rɒŋ (went, gɒn)/
reserve /rɪ'zɜːv/
examine /ɪg'zæmɪn/
repair /rɪ'peə(r)/
pleased /pliːzd/

Unit 18: Lesson A

Grammar and structures

Direct speech and reported speech
They thought 'The sun **goes** round the earth'.
They **thought** that the sun **went** round the earth.

   (**NOT** ~~They thought that the sun goes...~~)
Galileo said, 'Light and heavy things **fall** at the same speed'.
Galileo **said** that light and heavy things **fell** at the same speed.

Reported questions
They wondered **if/whether** Aristotle was right.
Do you know **whether** Britain has a king **or** a queen?
She asked **what my name was**.
   (**NOT** ~~what was my name.~~)
Do you know **where she lives**?
   (**NOT** ~~where does she live?~~)

Words and expressions to learn

the blood /ðə 'blʌd/
illness /'ɪlnɪs/
star /stɑː(r)/
scientist /'saɪəntɪst/
religion /rɪ'lɪdʒən/
politics /'pɒlətɪks/
war /wɔː(r)/
experiment /ɪks'perɪmənt/
cause /kɔːz/
tell a lie (told, told) /'tel ə 'laɪ (təʊld)/
discover /dɪs'kʌvə(r)/
flat /flæt/
living /'lɪvɪŋ/
impossible /ɪm'pɒsəbl/

Unit 18: Lesson B

Grammar and structures

Modal verbs: probability and certainty
It **must** be late – it's getting dark.
It **might** be true, but I don't think it is.
She **can't** be English – she's got a French accent.
'Who's at the door?' 'It **could** be the postman.'

Likely
I'm likely to be in London next Tuesday. Can I get you
   anything?
Do you think it**'s likely to rain**?
There is likely to be a meeting on Tuesday.
There are likely to be about 20 people at the meeting.

Say and *tell*
Fred **said** that he was a photographer.
Fred **told Janet** that he was a photographer.
   (NOT Fred told that...)
   (NOT Fred said Janet that...)

Words and expressions to learn
full name /'fʊl 'neɪm/
profession /prə'feʃn/
poetry /'pəʊətri/
parking place /'pɑːkɪŋ 'pleɪs/
photograph /'fəʊtəgrɑːf/
likely /'laɪkli/
none /nʌn/

Learn some words from the text about the Amazon Forest.

Revision vocabulary: do you know these words?

age /eɪdʒ/
address /ə'dres/
interest /'ɪntrəst/
education /edjʊ'keɪʃn/
qualifications /kwɒlɪfɪ'keɪʃnz/
spring /sprɪŋ/
phone call /'fəʊn 'kɔːl/
election /ɪ'lekʃn/
say (said, said) /seɪ (sed)/
tell (told, told) /tel (təʊld)/
travel /'trævl/
happen /'hæpn/
true /truː/
famous /'feɪməs/
strange /streɪndʒ/
wet /wet/
by (=not later than) /baɪ/

Unit 19: Lesson A

Grammar and structures

Question-tags
You're German, **aren't you?**
You've changed the room round, **haven't you?**
She can speak Arabic, **can't she?**
Your wife smokes, doesn't she?
The film started late, **didn't it?**

Place of prepositions in questions
What are you talking **about?**
   (NOT About what are you talking?)
What are you looking **at?**
Who did she go **with?**
Who are you looking **for?**

Words and expressions to learn
sofa /'səʊfə/
coat /kəʊt/
ground /graʊnd/
weekday /'wiːkdeɪ/
a change /ə 'tʃeɪndʒ/
move /muːv/
ask for /'ɑːsk fə(r)/
delicious /dɪ'lɪʃəs/
hard work
somewhere else
I beg your pardon? /aɪ 'beg jə 'pɑːdn/
I should think
How do you mean?

Could you pass me...
I've had enough
How stupid of me!

Learn two or more of these:
mustard /'mʌstəd/
meat /miːt/
bean /biːn/
carrot /'kærət/
wine /waɪn/

Unit 19: Lesson B

Grammar and structures

Agreeing and disagreeing with opinions
I like...	So do I.
I quite like...	I don't.
I really like...	I quite like him/her/
I like... very much.	it/them.
I love...	I've never heard of him/
	her/it/them.

So do I, Neither do I, etc.
'**I like** traditional jazz.' '**So do I.**'
'**I don't like** science fiction.' '**Neither do I.**'
'**Sarah is** tired.' '**So is Sally.**'
'**We're not** hungry.' '**Neither are we.**'
'**I've got** a headache.' '**So have I.**'
'**They haven't got** a car.' '**Neither have we.**'
'**Tim saw** Ann yesterday.' '**So did I.**'
'**I didn't have** a holiday last year.' '**Neither did I.**'
'**My brother will be** 35 next month.' '**So will I!**'
'**I won't be** here for the meeting.' '**Neither will I.**'
'**Tom was** fairer when he was a child.' '**So was Ruth.**'
'**You weren't** here when he came.' '**Neither were you.**'

Words and expressions to learn
sex /seks/
violence /'vaɪələns/
complete /kəm'pliːt/
awful /'ɔːfʊl/
old-fashioned /'əʊld 'fæʃənd/
whose /huːz/
I didn't think much of it.
I couldn't help it.
It's getting late.
We've got a long way to go.
We ought to be on our way.
I suppose
We'd better be going.
enjoy myself/yourself/etc.
Thank you for coming.
I'll give you a ring.
Thank you so much.

Revision vocabulary: do you know these words?
beginning /bɪ'gɪnɪŋ/
middle /'mɪdl/
end /end/
food /fuːd/
coffee /'kɒfi/
die /daɪ/
laugh /lɑːf/
spend (spent, spent) /spend (spent)/
dirty /'dɜːti/
mine /maɪn/
I can't stand...
See you next week.

Unit 20: Lesson A

Grammar and structures

Infinitive of purpose
To make tomatoes easier to peel, cover them...
   (NOT ~~For to make...~~)

By... ing
You can clean dirty saucepans **by filling** them
   with cold water and vinegar and letting them
   boil for five minutes.

Had better
I **had** (I'**d**) **better** phone my sister.
   (NOT ~~I'd better to phone...~~)
   (NOT ~~I have better...~~)
You **had** (You'**d**) **better** phone your sister. etc.

Had I **better** phone her now?
Had you **better** phone her now? etc.

I **had** (I'**d**) **better not** wait any longer.
   (NOT ~~I hadn't better...~~)
You **had** (you'**d**) **better not** wait any longer. etc.

Words and expressions to learn

finger /ˈfɪŋgə(r)/
rabbit /ˈræbɪt/
saucepan /ˈsɔːspən/
dust /dʌst/
rice /raɪs/
scratch /skrætʃ/
luggage /ˈlʌgɪdʒ/
examination /ɪgzæmɪˈneɪʃn/
peel /piːl/
rub /rʌb/
shake (shook, shaken) /ʃeɪk (ʃʊk, ˈʃeɪkn)/
stick (stuck, stuck) /stɪk (stʌk)/
catch (caught, caught) /kætʃ (kɔːt)/
empty /ˈempti/
tight /taɪt/
pregnant /ˈpregnənt/

Revision vocabulary: do you know these words?

tomato /təˈmɑːtəʊ/
guitar /gɪˈtɑː(r)/
glass /glɑːs/
newspaper /ˈnjuːspeɪpə(r)/
ear /ɪə(r)/
potato /pəˈteɪtəʊ/
apple /ˈæpl/
beer /bɪə(r)/
yard /jɑːd/
ring (rang, rung) /rɪŋ (ræŋ, rʌŋ)/
cover /ˈkʌvə(r)/
wash /wɒʃ/
pick up /ˈpɪk ˈʌp/
visit /ˈvɪzɪt/
dirty /ˈdɜːti/
together /təˈgeðə(r)/
comfortable /ˈkʌmftəbl/
wet /wet/

Unit 20: Lesson B

Grammar and structures

Suggestions
If I **were** you, I'**d** turn it the other way round.
I **think** you **ought to** turn it upside down.
Why don't you turn it sideways?
Let's help him.

If + 'unreal' conditions
If I **were** you, I'**d** (I **would**) turn it the other
   way round.
It **would be** much better if he **turned** it back
   to front.
What **would** you **do** if you **had** this mess in
   your kitchen?
I **wouldn't do** it like that if I **were** you.
Wouldn't you?

Ought to
You **ought to** turn it upside
   down.
She **ought to** be able to get
   one free.
   (NOT ~~She oughts to...~~)

Imperatives + *or*
Put a blanket underneath it
   or it'll get dirty.
Cover it **or** it'll get wet.

Remember to, forget to
Remember to cover it...
Don't **forget to** tighten all
   the screws.

Words and expressions to learn

screw /skruː/
law /lɔː/
drug /drʌg/
give up (gave, given) /ˈgɪv ˈʌp (geɪv, ˈgɪvn)/
seem /siːm/
immediately /ɪˈmiːdɪətli/
back to front /ˈbæk tə ˈfrʌnt/
face downwards /ˈfeɪs ˈdaʊnwədz/
inside out /ˈɪnsaɪd ˈaʊt/
sideways /ˈsaɪdweɪz/
underneath /ʌndəˈniːθ/
upside down /ˈʌpsaɪd ˈdaʊn/
the other way round /ði ˈʌðə ˈweɪ ˈraʊnd/
this way /ˈðɪs ˈweɪ/
I'll think about it. /aɪl ˈθɪŋk əˈbaʊt ɪt/
It's no trouble. /ɪts ˈnəʊ ˈtrʌbl/

Unit 21: Lesson A

Grammar and structures

Must and *mustn't*
·In Britain you **must** buy a licence if you have a TV.
   (NOT ~~...you must to buy...~~)
You **must** unplug an electrical appliance before you try
   to repair it.
You **mustn't** touch anything electrical if you are in
   the bath.

Phrasal verbs
Switch on the radio. **Switch** the radio **on**.
Switch it **on**. (NOT ~~Switch on it.~~)
Turn up the TV. **Turn** the TV **up**.
Turn it **up**. (NOT ~~Turn up it.~~)

Which (of)
Which would you choose?
Which colour would you like?

Which of the things in the picture would you like?
Which of them would you like?

Words and expressions to learn

plug in /ˈplʌg ˈɪn/
unplug /ʌnˈplʌg/
turn up /ˈtɜːn ˈʌp/
turn down /ˈtɜːn ˈdaʊn/

Learn some of these:

tape recorder /ˈteɪp rɪˈkɔːdə(r)/
stereo /ˈsterɪəʊ/
record player /ˈrekɔːd ˈpleɪə(r)/
cassette player /kəˈset ˈpleɪə(r)/
vacuum cleaner /ˈvækjuːəm ˈkliːnə(r)/
hair dryer /ˈheə ˈdraɪə(r)/
washing machine /ˈwɒʃɪŋ məˈʃiːn/

dishwasher /ˈdɪʃwɒʃə(r)/
mixer /ˈmɪksə(r)/
dryer /ˈdraɪə(r)/
heater /ˈhiːtə(r)/
cooker /ˈkʊkə(r)/
iron /ˈaɪən/
toaster /ˈtəʊstə(r)/
bulb /bʌlb/

knob /nɒb/
plug /plʌg/
socket /ˈsɒkɪt/
lead /liːd/
lamp /læmp/
torch /tɔːtʃ/
battery /ˈbætri/
wire /ˈwaɪə(r)/

149

Unit 21: Lesson B

Grammar and structures

Verb + *-ing* form
It's **started making** a funny noise.
It **keeps sticking**.
It won't **stop dripping**.

Won't
It **won't** start.

Words and expressions to learn

flash /flæʃ/
engine /'endʒən/
dial /daɪl/
record /rɪ'kɔ:d/
wind (wound, wound) /waɪnd (waʊnd)/
rewind (rewound, rewound)
  /ri:'waɪnd (ri:'waʊnd)/

flood /flʌd/
keep (kept, kept) /ki:p (kept)/
ring (rang, rung) /rɪŋ (ræŋ, rʌŋ)/
leak /li:k/
properly /'prɒpəli/
take a photo
there's something wrong with...

Unit 22: Lesson A

Spelling and pronunciation

Two syllables, not three: asp(i)rin, bus(i)ness, cam(e)ra, diff(e)rent, ev(e)ning, ev(e)ry, marri(a)ge, med(i)cine.

Three syllables, not four: comf(or)table, secret(a)ry, temp(e)rature, veg(e)table, usu(a)lly.

Silent letters: shou(l)d, cou(l)d, wou(l)d, ca(l)m, wa(l)k, ta(l)k, ha(l)f, i(r)on, i(s)land, lis(t)en, (w)rite, (w)rong, (k)now, (k)nife, (k)nee, (k)nock, (k)nob, dau(gh)ter, hei(gh)t, li(gh)t, mi(gh)t, ri(gh)t, ti(gh)t, strai(gh)t, throu(gh), wei(gh), nei(gh)bour, ou(gh)t, thou(gh)t, g(u)ess, g(u)ide, g(u)itar, (h)our, (h)onest, We(d)n(e)sday, san(d)wich, si(g)n.

gh = /f/	cough, enough, laugh.	
ch = /k/	chemist, headache, toothache, stomach, school, scheme.	
a = /e/	any, many	
ea = /e/	bread, breakfast, dead, death, head, health, heavy, instead, leather, pleasure, ready, sweater.	
ea = /eɪ/	steak, break.	
o = /ʌ/	brother, come, company, cover, government, love, money, month, mother, nothing, one, onion, other, some, son, stomach, wonder, worry.	
ou = /ʌ/	country, couple, cousin, double, enough, trouble.	
u = /ʊ/	butcher, pull, push, put.	

All these words are pronounced with /aɪ/: dial, either, neither, buy, height, idea, iron, microphone.

Strange spellings:

area /'eərɪə/
Asia /'eɪʃə/
Australia /ɒs'treɪlɪə/
autumn /'ɔ:təm/
bicycle /'baɪsɪkl/
blood /blʌd/
biscuit /'bɪskɪt/
busy /'bɪzi/

Europe /'jʊərəp/
foreign /'fɒrən/
friend /frend/
fruit /fru:t/
heard /hɜ:d/
heart /hɑ:t/
juice /dʒu:s/
minute /'mɪnɪt/

moustache /mə'stɑ:ʃ/
one /wʌn/
people /'pi:pl/
sandwich /'sænwɪdʒ/
theatre /'θɪətə(r)/
two /tu:/
woman /'wʊmən/
women /'wɪmɪn/

> THERE IS NO SUMMARY FOR
> UNIT 22, LESSON B

Additional material

Lesson 13A, Exercise 10

The Island

Each night I dream of a beautiful island
Surrounded by beaches and covered in flowers.
Butterflies dance through the sweet-smelling meadows
And birds sing their love songs for hours.

Crystal clear water runs down from the mountains
And flows through deep valleys as a sparkling stream.
Gentle sea breezes blow over my island
While sunshine pours over my dream.

> Each night I visit the island of my dreams,
> Each night I visit the island of my dreams,
> I leave the real world behind,
> It's somewhere deep in my mind,
> Not too easy to find,
> The island.

Bright orange squirrels play games in the tree tops
And chase through the branches where nightingales sing.
It looks so peaceful I wish I could take you
To where each night's the first day of spring.

Chorus.

> I leave the real world behind,
> It's somewhere deep in my mind,
> Not too easy to find,
> The island.

The island.   The island.

Jonathan Dykes (lyrics)
Robert Campbell (music)

Lesson 14B, Dialogue B

MOTHER: Can I speak to you for a minute, Em?
DAUGHTER: . . . .
MOTHER: Well, I'm very upset about how late you were
            out last night.
DAUGHTER: . . . .
MOTHER: I still think that's too late for a fifteen-year-old
            girl who has to go to school the next day.
DAUGHTER: . . . .
MOTHER: Well, you're not all the other kids. And I'm sure
            some of them have to be in early.
DAUGHTER: . . . .
MOTHER: Especially on school nights. I don't want you in
            after ten when you've got school the next day.
DAUGHTER: . . . .
MOTHER: Well, if there's a special night we can talk about
            it before you go. I'm sure we can agree if we
            talk about it.
DAUGHTER: . . . .
MOTHER: Thanks, darling.

Unit 19 Dialogues

DIALOGUE 1

(The doorbell rings.)

PETER: I'll go.
ANN: OK.

(Peter opens the door.)

PETER: Hello, hello. Nice to see you.
SUE: Hello, Peter. Are we late?
PETER: No, not at all. You're the first, actually.
JOHN: Oh, good. Who else is coming?
PETER: Come in and have a drink. Well, there's Don and
        Emma, Jo and Stephen, and my sister Lucy and her
        new boyfriend. Can't remember his name. Let me
        take your coat. You know Lucy, don't you?
SUE: I think we've met her once.
ANN: Hello, Sue. Hello, John. Lovely to see you. I'm so
        glad you could come. Now, what can I get you to
        drink?
SUE: What have you got?
ANN: Oh, the usual things. Sherry; gin and tonic – I think;
        vodka; I think there's some beer; a glass of
        wine . . . ?
SUE: I'll have a gin and tonic, Ann, please.
JOHN: So will I.
SUE: Doesn't the room look nice, John? You've changed it
        round since we were here last, haven't you? The
        piano was, let me see, yes, the piano was over by
        the window, wasn't it?
PETER: That's right. And we've moved the sofa over there
        and . . .

DIALOGUE 2

JOHN: So you work in a pub.
LUCY: Yes, that's right.
JOHN: What's it like?
LUCY: It's nice. I like it. You meet a lot of interesting
        people. A lot of boring ones too, mind you.
JOHN: I beg your pardon?
LUCY: I said, a lot of boring ones too.
JOHN: Oh, yes. I can imagine. A pub – I should think that's
        hard work, isn't it?
LUCY: Yes and no. It depends.
JOHN: How do you mean?
LUCY: Well, it's hard at weekends. I mean, last Saturday
        night, with both bars full and one barman away ill –
        well, my feet didn't touch the ground. But on
        weekdays it's usually very quiet.
        What about you? What do you do? You're an
        accountant or something, aren't you?
JOHN: I work in a bank.
LUCY: Oh yes, that's right. Ann said. That must be nice.
JOHN: It's all right.
LUCY: But you have to move round from one place to
        another, don't you? I mean, if you get a better job – if
        they make you manager or something – it'll probably
        be in another town, won't it?
JOHN: Yes, probably.
LUCY: I wouldn't like that. I mean, I've got lots of friends
        here. I wouldn't like to move somewhere else.
JOHN: Oh, we like it. We've lived here for, what, six years
        now. We're ready for a change.

DIALOGUE 3

DON:	Have you got the salt down your end, Steve?
STEPHEN:	What are you looking for?
DON:	The salt.
STEPHEN:	Salt. Salt. Oh, yes. Here it is. And could you pass me the mustard in exchange? This is delicious beef, Ann. Who's your butcher?
ANN:	Not telling you. What are John and Lucy talking about?
JOHN:	Work, I'm afraid.
SUE:	I thought so. It's all John ever talks about. Work and food.
JOHN:	Well, there are worse things in life. Especially if the food's like this.
ANN:	Thank you, John. Would you like some more? Have another potato. Some more meat. Some beans. A carrot. A piece of bread.
JOHN:	No, thanks. That was lovely, but I've had enough. Really. I'll have another glass of wine, perhaps.
EMMA:	Here you are, John.

(Crash!)

	Oh, damn! I *am* sorry, Ann. How stupid of me.
ANN:	That's all right. It doesn't matter at all. Really. They're very cheap glasses.

DIALOGUE 4

ANDY:	I didn't like it at all.
EMMA:	Oh, I thought it was lovely.
JOHN:	It was rubbish. Complete rubbish. Absolute nonsense.
ANN:	I didn't think much of it, I must say.
LUCY:	I liked it. At the end, when she was dying, I cried. I couldn't help it. I cried and cried.
STEPHEN:	Jo said it made her laugh.
JO:	No, I didn't. Oh, Steve, you are awful! Really! No, it's just that – I don't know – it didn't say anything to me.
JOHN:	I'm afraid I must be very old-fashioned, but I like things to have a beginning, a middle and an end.
STEPHEN:	Yes, so do I.
JOHN:	And I *don't* like a lot of sex and violence.
EMMA:	Oh, I love sex and violence!
ANN:	More coffee, anybody?
ANDY:	I don't like violence.
EMMA:	But listen. Why didn't you like it? I thought it was great. Really.
ANN:	So wordy. It was really really boring. They just talked and talked and talked all the time.
STEPHEN:	I can't stand –
EMMA:	No, look –
LUCY:	I don't think –
DON:	Three old women sitting around talking for two and a half hours. If that's what you want, you might as well go and spend the evening in the old people's home.
LUCY:	It wasn't like that at all.
ANDY:	Yes it was.
LUCY:	No it wasn't.
ANDY:	Yes it was.
ANN :	Who wrote it, anyway?
JO:	Don't know. What's his name? Fred Walker, something like that.
ANDY:	Who's he?
DON:	Never heard of him.
STEPHEN:	Didn't he write . . .

DIALOGUE 5

DON:	Well, I'm afraid it's getting late, and we've got a long way to go.
SUE:	So have we. We ought to be on our way, I suppose.
JO:	Yes, we'd better be going, too. Thank you so much, Ann. We really enjoyed ourselves. Lovely food, nice people, good talk, . . .
ANN:	Well, thank you for coming.
EMMA:	You must come over to us soon. When we've finished moving. I'll give you a ring.
JOHN:	Now, where's my coat?
PETER:	Here it is, John.
JOHN:	No, that's not mine. This is mine.
PETER:	Oh, sorry. Well, whose is this, then?
ANN:	Andy's, I think.
ANDY:	Is it old and dirty? Yes, that's mine.
LUCY:	Well, bye, Ann, bye, Peter. See you next week.
EVERYBODY:	Bye, bye.

Lesson 14B, Dialogue A

MOTHER:	....
DAUGHTER:	Sure, Mum, what's the problem?
MOTHER:	....
DAUGHTER:	But Mum, I was in by twelve o'clock!
MOTHER:	....
DAUGHTER:	Well, I don't think so. All the other kids stay out late.
MOTHER:	....
DAUGHTER:	Yeah, some of them do, I suppose.
MOTHER:	....
DAUGHTER:	But last night was special. It was the disco at the club.
MOTHER:	....
DAUGHTER:	All right, Mum. Perhaps you're right. I'll talk to you about it next time.
MOTHER:	....

Acknowledgements

The authors and publishers are grateful to the following copyright owners for permission to reproduce photographs, illustrations, texts and music. Every endeavour has been made to contact copyright owners and apologies are expressed for any omissions.

page 21: Reproduced by permission of Syndication International. page 31: Reproduced by permission of *Punch*. page 39: Reproduced by permission of British Telecom. page 60: *cl* 'My mother said...' from *God Bless Love*, Nanette Newman (Collins, 1972), © Invalid Children's Association, reproduced by kind permission of ICA. *tc, br* 'Dear God...', 'If they don't want...' from *Children's Letters to God* (Fontana, Collins, 1976), reproduced by permission of the Publisher. *cr* 'My mum only likes...' from Extracts from Nanette Newman's Collections of Sayings, by permission of the authors, © reserved. page 61: From Extracts from Nanette Newman's Collection of Sayings, by permission of the authors, © reserved. page 92: *tr* Courtesy of John, Hairdresser, Croydon, *cr* Mobil Oil Company Limited. page 93: *tr* Courtesy of Joan Galleli, The Shirley Poppy. page 96: *b* Reproduced by permission of *Punch*. page 98: From the *Longman Active Study Dictionary of English* edited by Della Summers, Longman 1983. page 102: *tr* Photographie Musée National d'Art Moderne, Centre Georges Pompidou, Paris. *tl* Reproduced by courtesy of the Trustees, The National Gallery, London. *bl* Reproduced by courtesy of the Board of Trustees of the Victoria and Albert Museum. page 104: *l* Courtesy of Gallery Lingard. *r* Reproduced from the poster of the London Mozart Players 1984–1985. *c* Reproduced from London Features International Ltd. page 113: From an article by Anna Tomforde in the *Guardian* – adapted. page 115: Reproduced by permission of *Punch*. page 116: *t* Reproduced by permission of *Punch*. *b* From *Weekend Book of Jokes 21* (Harmsworth Publications Ltd.), reproduced by permission of Associated Newspapers Plc. page 117: Reproduced by permission of Syndication International. page 124: 'My dad...', 'A prime minister...' 'When you grow up...' Reproduced by permission of Bryan Forbes Ltd. page 128: Nos. 1-7, 10 from *The Highway Code* (Her Majesty's Stationery Office), Reproduced by permission of the Publisher. Colour details: 1. green light showing. Other lights are red (top) and amber (middle). 2. same as (1) except that red light is showing. 3. red triangle, white background, black letters. 4. white circle, red background, white horizontal line. 5. red circle and diagonal, white background, black directional sign. 6. red circle, white background, black man. 7. red triangle, white background, black car and lines. 8. grey road, yellow double lines, white dotted lines. 9. grey road, white lines. 10. red triangle, white background, black rocks. page 131: *tl* McLachlan. *tr, c, bl* Reproduced by permission of *Punch*. *br* Reproduced by permission of Syndication International. page 156: Song *You Made Me Love You*, lyrics: Joe McCarthy, music: James V. Monaco. © 1913 Broadway Music Corp, USA. Sub-published by Francis Day & Hunter Ltd., London WC2H 0LD. Reproduced by permission of EMI Music Publishing Ltd. and International Music Publications. page 158: Song *Trying to Love Two Women*, by Sonny Throckmorton, © Cross Keys Publishing Company Inc., USA. Sub-published by EMI Music Publishing Ltd., London WC2H 0LD. Reproduced by permission of EMI Publishing Ltd. and International Music Publications. page 158: Song *The Riddle Song* by Harry Robinson & Julie Felix, © 1965 TRO Essex Music Ltd., Bury Place, London WC1A 2LA for the World International Copyright secured. All Rights Reserved. page 159: The version of the song *Logger Lover* is by Dick Stephenson and is used with permission. page 159: *What Did You Learn in School Today?*, words and music by Tom Paxton. Reprinted by permission of Harmony Music Limited, 19/20 Poland Street, London W1V 3DD.

The songs *Brighton in the Rain* (Lesson 7A, page 156), *Song for a Rainy Sunday* (Lesson 10A, page 156), *The Island* (Lesson 13A, page 156), *My Old Dad* (Lesson 14A, page 59), *Another Street Incident* (Lesson 17B, page 72), and *A Bigger Heart* (Lesson 22A, page 90) were specially written for *The Cambridge English Course* Book 2 by Jonathan Dykes (lyrics) and Robert Campbell (music). The recorded material for Lesson 11A, Exercise 4 (page 181) and Revision Tests 1 (page 166) and 2 (page 170) is used by kind permission of Wiltshire Radio.

Ace Photo Agency: p92 *l*. BBC Hulton Picture Library: p110 *br*. Camera Press Limited: p110 *tr*, nos. 2, 3, *c* (Margaret Thatcher), *b* (second from *l*). The Daily Telegraph: pages 98 *l*, 122 (teacher, farmer, 3 industrial photos). p50: *tc* Courtesy of Jaakko Poyry (UK) Limited. London Features International Limited: p104 *c*. Monitor Picture Library: p93 *tl, br*. Pictorial Press Limited: p110 *b* (second from *r*). Alan Philip: pages 6–7, 36, 64. The Press Association: p95 *t*. Doc Rowe: p105. Spectrum Colour Library: pages 36–37, 98 *r*. Sporting Pictures UK Limited: p95 *b*. Syndication International Limited: pages 110 *tc, cr*, nos. 1, 4, *bl*, 122 (housewife, nurse). John Topham Picture Library: pages 68, 74–75. p125: © United Kingdom Atomic Energy Authority, used with permission. Reg van Cuÿlenburg: pages 22, 63, 66–67. Catherine Walter: p8. Wiggins Teape Group: p50 *tr, br*. Jason Youé: pages 92 *tr, cr*, 93 *tr, cl, cr*, 125 *t*.

John Craddock: Malcolm Barter, pages 14 *t*, 37 *b*, 38–39, 58, 69 *b*, 78–79, 80–81; Alexa Rutherford, pages 20, 28, 59, 94, 108 *t*, 120; Kate Simunek, p57; Ian Fleming and Associates Limited: Terry Burton, p100; David Lewis Management: Odette Buchanan, pages 18, 45, 91, 112; Bob Harvey, pages 40, 41 *r*, 65, 69 *t*, 72, 88, 113, 121 *r*; Jon Miller, pages 10–11, 84, 121 *b*; Linda Rogers: Mike Whittlesea, pages 27, 44 *b*, 71 *l*, 82 *t*, 108 *b*, 114 *t*; Linden Artists Limited: Jon Davis, pages 30 *b*, 35, 70, 126–127; Val Sangster, pages 16, 24, 71 *r*, 96 *t*, 114 *b*.

Paul Davenport, pages 44 *t*, 52–53, 76; Paul Francis, pages 14 *b*, 15; Martin Gordon, p42; Gary Inwood, pages 41 *l*, 43, 73, 82 *b*, 123; Jane Molineaux, pages 26, 77; Chris Rawlings, pages 30 *t*, 33; Nik Spender, pages 12–13, 56, 83, 118, 132–133; Tony Streek, pages 23, 34, 54 *t*, 89, 119; Malcolm Ward, pages 19, 54 *b*, 86, 109, 111; Jack Wood, pages 51, 54 *b*, 55, 112; Mike Woodhatch, pages 106–107; John Youé & Associates.

(Abbreviations: *t*=top *b*=bottom *c*=centre *r*=right *l*=left)

Phonetic symbols

Vowels

symbol	example	symbol	example
/i:/	eat /i:t/	/eɪ/	day /deɪ/
/i/	happy /'hæpi/	/aɪ/	my /maɪ/
/ɪ/	it /ɪt/	/ɔɪ/	boy /bɔɪ/
/e/	when /wen/	/aʊ/	now /naʊ/
/æ/	cat /kæt/	/əʊ/	go /gəʊ/
/ɑ:/	hard /hɑ:d/	/ɪə/	here /hɪə(r)/
/ɒ/	not /nɒt/	/eə/	chair /tʃeə(r)/
/ɔ:/	sort /sɔ:t/; all /ɔ:l/	/ʊə/	tour /tʊə(r)/
/ʊ/	look /lʊk/		
/u:/	too /tu:/		
/ʌ/	up /ʌp/		
/ɜ:/	bird /bɜ:d/; turn /tɜ:n/		
/ə/	about /ə'baʊt/; mother /'mʌðə(r)/		

Consonants

symbol	example	symbol	example
/p/	pen /pen/	/h/	who /hu:/; how /haʊ/
/b/	big /bɪg/	/m/	meet /mi:t/
/t/	two /tu:/	/n/	no /nəʊ/
/d/	do /du:/	/ŋ/	sing /sɪŋ/
/k/	look /lʊk/; cup /kʌp/	/l/	long /lɒŋ/
/g/	get /get/	/r/	right /raɪt/
/tʃ/	China /'tʃaɪnə/	/j/	yet /jet/
/dʒ/	Japan /dʒə'pæn/	/w/	will /wɪl/
/f/	fall /fɔ:l/		
/v/	very /'veri/		
/θ/	think /θɪŋk/		
/ð/	then /ðen/		
/s/	see /si:/		
/z/	zoo /zu:/; is /ɪz/		
/ʃ/	shoe /ʃu:/		
/ʒ/	pleasure /'pleʒə(r)/; decision /dɪ'sɪʒn/		

Stress

Stress is shown by a mark (') in front of the stressed syllable.

mother /'mʌðə(r)/
about /ə'baʊt/
China /'tʃaɪnə/
Japan /dʒə'pæn/

Irregular verbs

Infinitive	Simple Past	Past Participle
be /bi:/	was /wəz, wɒz/	been /bɪn, bi:n/
	were /wə, wɜ:(r)/	
beat /bi:t/	beat /bi:t/	beaten /'bi:tn/
become /bɪ'kʌm/	became /bɪ'keɪm/	become /bɪ'kʌm/
begin /bɪ'gɪn/	began /bɪ'gæn/	begun /bɪ'gʌn/
bend /bend/	bent /bent/	bent /bent/
bet /bet/	bet /bet/	bet /bet/
bite /baɪt/	bit /bɪt/	bitten /'bɪtn/
bleed /bli:d/	bled /bled/	bled /bled/
break /breɪk/	broke /brəʊk/	broken /'brəʊkn/
bring /brɪŋ/	brought /brɔ:t/	brought /brɔ:t/
build /bɪld/	built /bɪlt/	built /bɪlt/
burn /bɜ:n/	burnt /bɜ:nt/	burnt /bɜ:nt/
buy /baɪ/	bought /bɔ:t/	bought /bɔ:t/
catch /kætʃ/	caught /kɔ:t/	caught /kɔ:t/
choose /tʃu:z/	chose /tʃəʊz/	chosen /'tʃəʊzn/
come /kʌm/	came /keɪm/	come /kʌm/
cost /kɒst/	cost /kɒst/	cost /kɒst/
cut /kʌt/	cut /kʌt/	cut /kʌt/
deal /di:l/	dealt /delt/	dealt /delt/
do /dʊ, də, du:/	did /dɪd/	done /dʌn/
draw /drɔ:/	drew /dru:/	drawn /drɔ:n/
dream /dri:m/	dreamt /dremt/	dreamt /dremt/
drink /drɪŋk/	drank /dræŋk/	drunk /drʌŋk/
drive /draɪv/	drove /drəʊv/	driven /'drɪvn/
eat /i:t/	ate /et/	eaten /'i:tn/
fall /fɔ:l/	fell /fel/	fallen /'fɔ:lən/
feel /fi:l/	felt /felt/	felt /felt/
find /faɪnd/	found /faʊnd/	found /faʊnd/
fly /flaɪ/	flew /flu:/	flown /fləʊn/
forget /fə'get/	forgot /fə'gɒt/	forgotten /fə'gɒtn/
get /get/	got /gɒt/	got /gɒt/
give /gɪv/	gave /geɪv/	given /'gɪvn/
go /gəʊ/	went /went/	gone /gɒn/
		been /bɪn, bi:n/
grow /grəʊ/	grew /gru:/	grown /grəʊn/
have /həv, hæv/	had /(h)əd, hæd/	had /hæd/
hear /hɪə(r)/	heard /hɜ:d/	heard /hɜ:d/
hide /haɪd/	hid /hɪd/	hidden /'hɪdn/
hit /hɪt/	hit /hɪt/	hit /hɪt/
hurt /hɜ:t/	hurt /hɜ:t/	hurt /hɜ:t/
keep /ki:p/	kept /kept/	kept /kept/
know /nəʊ/	knew /nju:/	known /nəʊn/
lead /li:d/	led /led/	led /led/
learn /lɜ:n/	learnt /lɜ:nt/	learnt /lɜ:nt/
leave /li:v/	left /left/	left /left/
lend /lend/	lent /lent/	lent /lent/
let /let/	let /let/	let /let/
lie /laɪ/	lay /leɪ/	lain /leɪn/
lose /lu:z/	lost /lɒst/	lost /lɒst/
make /meɪk/	made /meɪd/	made /meɪd/
mean /mi:n/	meant /ment/	meant /ment/

Infinitive	Simple Past	Past Participle
meet /mi:t/	met /met/	met /met/
pay /peɪ/	paid /peɪd/	paid /peɪd/
put /pʊt/	put /pʊt/	put /pʊt/
read /ri:d/	read /red/	read /red/
rewind /ri:'waɪnd/	rewound /ri:'waʊnd/	rewound /ri:'waʊnd/
ride /raɪd/	rode /rəʊd/	ridden /'rɪdn/
ring /rɪŋ/	rang /ræŋ/	rung /rʌŋ/
rise /raɪz/	rose /rəʊz/	risen /'rɪzn/
run /rʌn/	ran /ræn/	run /rʌn/
say /seɪ/	said /sed/	said /sed/
see /si:/	saw /sɔ:/	seen /si:n/
sell /sel/	sold /səʊld/	sold /səʊld/
send /send/	sent /sent/	sent /sent/
shake /ʃeɪk/	shook /ʃʊk/	shaken /'ʃeɪkn/
show /ʃəʊ/	showed /ʃəʊd/	shown /ʃəʊn/
shrink /ʃrɪŋk/	shrank /ʃræŋk/	shrunk /ʃrʌŋk/
shut /ʃʌt/	shut /ʃʌt/	shut /ʃʌt/
sing /sɪŋ/	sang /sæŋ/	sung /sʌŋ/
sit /sɪt/	sat /sæt/	sat /sæt/
sleep /sli:p/	slept /slept/	slept /slept/
smell /smel/	smelt /smelt/	smelt /smelt/
speak /spi:k/	spoke /spəʊk/	spoken /'spəʊkn/
spell /spel/	spelt /spelt/	spelt /spelt/
spend /spend/	spent /spent/	spent /spent/
spill /spɪl/	spilt /spɪlt/	spilt /spɪlt/
stand /stænd/	stood /stʊd/	stood /stʊd/
steal /sti:l/	stole /stəʊl/	stolen /'stəʊlən/
stick /stɪk/	stuck /stʌk/	stuck /stʌk/
swim /swɪm/	swam /swæm/	swum /swʌm/
take /teɪk/	took /tʊk/	taken /'teɪkn/
teach /ti:tʃ/	taught /tɔ:t/	taught /tɔ:t/
tell /tel/	told /təʊld/	told /təʊld/
think /θɪŋk/	thought /θɔ:t/	thought /θɔ:t/
throw /θrəʊ/	threw /θru:/	thrown /θrəʊn/
understand /ʌndə'stænd/	understood /ʌndə'stʊd/	understood /ʌndə'stʊd/
wake up /'weɪk 'ʌp/	woke up /'wəʊk 'ʌp/	woken up /'wəʊkn 'ʌp/
wear /weə(r)/	wore /wɔ:(r)/	worn /wɔ:n/
win /wɪn/	won /wʌn/	won /wʌn/
wind /waɪnd/	wound /waʊnd/	wound /waʊnd/
write /raɪt/	wrote /rəʊt/	written /'rɪtn/